ThE
SECRI
OF
PLANETARY
MAGIC

ChRISTOPhER WARNOCK ESQ

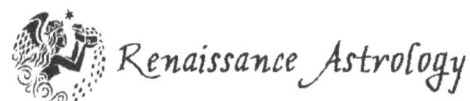 *Renaissance Astrology*

2010

ISBN 978-0-557-36626-2

Renaissance Astrology Press
www.renaissanceastrology.com

Renaissance Astrology

TO
KATHLEEN

CONTENTS

1

SECRETS of PLANETARY MAGIC

This book is the product of more than a decade of study and practice of traditional (pre-1700) astrology and magic, which involved reading traditional sources, translating Latin astrological magic texts, creating astrological talismans, performing rituals and observing the results. My quest has not been to create my own individual system or invent new methods, but rather to become another link in the Golden Chain of Western esoteric practice, to immerse myself in the ancient Hermetic and Neo-platonic philosophies which form the basis of traditional astrology and astrological magic, and to practice astrological magic and astrology using the techniques and methodologies of our illustrious, pre-"Enlightenment" predecessors.

Of necessity we must fill in the blanks where the sources are silent and we cannot nor is it desirable that we attempt to turn ourselves into exact copies of the mages of the Middle Ages and Renaissance. However, by first following the rules laid down in the traditional sources and then assimilating their essence, we can follow in the quest for magical knowledge and true spiritual enlightenment.

Much of this book is taken up with the nuts and bolts of planetary magic, but I would like to begin with what might, without much exaggeration, be termed the secrets of planetary magic.

These secrets are not tips, hints or recipes, but insights gleaned from years of study and practice.

The first and most important of the secrets of planetary magic is the existence and reality of the spiritual realm. Magic and astrology depend on the spiritual connection of all things. Without a firm grounding in the spiritual, planetary magic will be weak and ineffectual.

Secondly, while the creation of talismans can be viewed as the process of charging them with some form of energy, it appears to be more effective to view the process as an interaction with spiritual beings, in this case, the spirits, intelligences or archangels of the planets. The creation of talismans, says the ancient grimoire of astrological magic, the *Picatrix*, involves the action of spirit on body.[1] The process of creating a talisman is the process of ensoulment as we invite the spirit of the desired planet to dwell in and vivify the talisman.

This leads us to the third secret of planetary magic and indeed the use of the planets in traditional astrology. It is helpful to conceive of the planets as individual persons with their own distinct personalities. We will discuss planetary rulership later in this book and we can grasp the nature of each planet more swiftly if we view them as individuals with likes and dislikes, moods, qualities, attributes, strengths and weaknesses. This is also the best way to approach the planets in ritual. When we invoke the planets we are raising ourselves up to their spheres, opening up a door to their realm. The wise mage interacts with the planetary spirits in a respectful way. These are not Goetic spirits to be commanded, bargained with, or that require a protective circle, but rather angelic beings who may have unpleasant work to perform at times, but who have no rancor towards us, so long as we approach them properly.

Further revelations flow from this premise. Since the action of talismans is to open the realms and influences of the planets to us, then in many respects astrological magic is different from spell casting. The power of talismans is primarily external to the mage and the effect of a talisman will always be appropriate to the planet involved, but cannot necessarily be predicted or willed by the magician.

Another key revelation is that creating and maintaining a relationship with the spirits of the planets greatly increases the

---

[1] *Picatrix*, Bk I, ch. 2.

power of planetary magic and talismans. For example, I do a daily invocation of the planet that rules the day, as well as regular invocations of the spirits of particular talismans. Repeated ritual with a talisman creates a strong spiritual bond between you and the planetary spirit of that talisman. Along these same lines, you will have an easier time doing planetary magic using planets that are dignified in your birth chart because you already have a bond to these planets.[2]

Finally, the planetary spirits demand to be approached on their own terms and in particular at their preferred times. We cannot make an astrological talismans whenever we wish, but must wait until an astrologically auspicious moment arrives. The design and materials of a talisman are of minor importance, while the timing and ritual consecration are paramount. Astrological magic in general and planetary magic in particular depend on precise astrological timing. Without first mastering traditional (pre-1700) astrology, attempts to create planetary talismans will frequently be ineffectual and may even be counterproductive.

---

[2] *Picatrix*, Bk I, ch 5.

II

ThE PLANETS

The seven traditional planets, Saturn, Jupiter, Mars, the Sun, Venus, Mercury and the Moon, are a key part of astrology and astrological magic. The word astrology itself comes from the Greek *astro*, star and *logos*, speech, ratio or pattern. Thus astrology literally means the speech or pattern of the stars. Since the dawn of civilization in Babylonia and Chaldea, astrologers and magicians observed the cycles of the Heavens, with a strong focus on the planets, and used them to predict and influence events on Earth. Astrology flourished during periods of high civilization: among the Greeks and Romans, the advanced Islamic civilization of the Middle East, and in Europe in the Middle Ages and Renaissance. The astrology practiced during this last period, approximately A.D. 1200-1700, is known as traditional astrology. Unlike the predominately psychologically oriented modern astrology, traditional astrology emphasizes prediction and providing definitive answers to specific questions, and traditional astrological magic focuses on the use of astrology for talismanic magic.

Our first question must be, how do astrology and magic work? This raises the issue of world view. A person's world view generally is some blend of the prevailing cultural world view and the person's own conscious philosophy and unconscious views about the nature of reality. In essence it is your reality. World view is so ingrained and automatic in our psyche that it is difficult for many to accept that anyone could have a different one. After all reality is reality, isn't it? It can be difficult to comprehend that other societies could have a radically different view of reality and even more difficult not to immediately reject that view as erroneous.

For our purposes, the key tenet of the modern world view is that nothing truly exists except matter and energy. For moderns, even when dealing with spiritual issues, their unconscious assumptions are always pushing towards atheistic materialism. When it comes to astrology, the automatic assumption is that the influence of the stars and planets must, of necessity, be exerted by matter or energy, i.e., some sort of electromagnetic field or rays, emanating from the stars and planets themselves. In fact, this is demonstrably false. There is simply no "scientific" evidence that explains how astrology or magic work, that is to say, there is no evidence that there is a material cause connecting cycles of the Heavens and events on Earth.

However, ancient and traditional astrologers did not have the modern world view. While there was of course much individual variation and change over time, the traditional world view saw reality as containing both the material and the spiritual. A typical formulation saw reality as composed of three worlds, the Divine or Angelic World of the Platonic Ideas and Archetypes, the Material World, and the intermediate Celestial World, where the material things lose their physicality and the Divine Ideas or Angels assume form. The entire Cosmos was seen as one great unified Being, bound together with chains of spiritual sympathy and correspondence. Matter was less perfect than the spiritual and thus imperfectly reflected the forms of the Divine/Platonic Ideas, which were the ultimate reality. Material things were created, changed their form and then passed away, while the spiritual was eternal. The ancient astrologers used their astrology to look through matter to see the hidden true spiritual patterns of reality. The impressive accuracy of traditional astrological prediction and the efficacy of astrological magic supports their world view as valid.

Each of the three worlds interpenetrates the others. For example, the Divine Idea of Justice appears in the Celestial World as Jupiter and in the Material World as just judges, lawyers and lawmakers. The Florentine philosopher and astrologer, Marsilio Ficino explains how things in each of the Worlds are connected through the Great Chain, or more precisely, the various chains of Being:

I have said elsewhere that down from every single star (so to speak Platonically) there hangs its own series of things down to the lowest...Under the celestial Serpent or the entire constellation of the Serpent-bearer, they place Saturn and sometimes Jupiter, afterwards daemons who often take on serpent's form, in addition men of this kind, serpents (the animals), the snake-weed, the stone draconite which originates in the head of a dragon, and the stone commonly called serpentine... By a similar system they think a chain of beings descends by levels from any star of the firmament through any planet under its dominion. If, therefore, as I said, you combine at the right time all the Solar things through any level of that order, i.e., men of Solar nature or something belonging to such a man, likewise animals, plants, metals, gems and whatever pertains to these, you will drink in unconditionally the power of the Sun and to some extent the natural powers of the Solar daemons.[3]

Everything is thus part of multiple chains of spiritual sympathy and correspondence connecting and interpenetrating all levels of reality. The seven traditional planets, Saturn, Jupiter, Mars, the Sun, Venus, Mercury and the Moon are key links in the Great Chain of Being. We can classify anything material under the rulership of one or more planets because the material thing contains the Divine idea or archetype transmitted by the planet. The Lion, for example, is the king of beasts and therefore ruled by the Sun, the King of the Planets. Gold is ruled also by the Sun because of its color, value and associations with kingship. Note however, that many things share multiple rulerships. While the Sun is the primary ruler of gold, Jupiter and Saturn also share rulership because gold, like Jupiter, is temperate and like Saturn, is heavy.

The Renaissance philosopher and mage Cornelius Agrippa explains:

Moreover whatsoever is found in the whole world is made according to the governments of the Planets, and accordingly receives its vertue. So in Fire the enlivening light thereof is under the government of the Sun, the heat of it under Mars, in the Earth, the various superficies thereof under the Moon, and Mercury; and the

---

[3] Marsilio Ficino, *Three Books on Life*, Book III, Chapter 14.

starry Heaven, the whole mass of it under Saturne, but in the middle Elements, Aire is under Jupiter, and Water the Moon, but being mixed are under Mercury, and Venus. ...Also amongst Vegetables, every thing that bears fruit is from Jupiter, and every thing that bears Flowers is from Venus, all Seed, and Bark is from Mercury, and all roots from Saturne, and all Wood from Mars, and leaves from the Moon. Wherefore, all that bring forth fruit, and not Flowers, are of Saturne and Jupiter, but they that bring forth Flowers, and Seed, and not fruit, are of Venus, and Mercury; These which are brought forth of their own accord without Seed, are of the Moon, and Saturn...[4]

In fact, all material things are connected to all of the planets. Planetary rulership is basically a way of stating which planet or planets predominate in the thing and very much depends on what part or quality we are focusing on. A helpful way to understand the nature of the planets is to read through the various rulership lists provided in Appendices A & B.

An astrologer's clear understanding of the natures of the planets is of considerable practical use. This knowledge is key for the interpretation of all types of horoscopes, particularly in the choice of significators. In horary astrology, which looks at the chart of the asking of a question rather than a birth chart, we can use the natures of the planets to obtain physical descriptions of suspected thieves or even casters of malefic spells. In electional astrology we can use planetary rulerships to determine whether a particular time is auspicious for a marriage that will result in children or a harmonious relationship. These examples are all passive uses of the planetary rulerships, where the astrologer observes the effects of the chains of correspondence and harmony. By contrast, in the practice of astrological magic, the mage or astrological magician makes active use of the planetary rulerships to create material effects.

---

[4] Cornelius Agrippa, *Three Books of Occult Philosophy*, Book I, Chapter 30.

III

PLANETARY SPHERES & PLANETARY HOURS

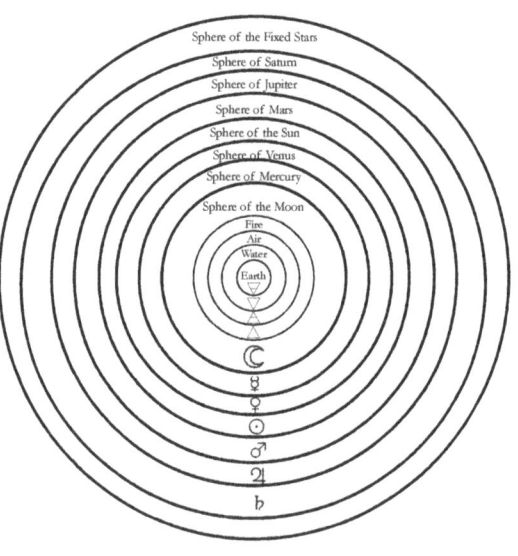

Traditional astrology saw the Cosmos arranged in a series of eight spheres which carefully fit inside each other. The highest sphere was that of the fixed stars and constellations. This sphere was moved by the *Primum Mobile*, the First Mover, which is an aspect of God. Surrounding everything was the Empyrean, the Divine heavens. The highest planetary sphere was that of Saturn, then Jupiter, Mars, the Sun, Venus, Mercury and the lowest sphere that of the Moon.

We note that the order of the planetary spheres follows the speed of the orbits of the planets. Saturn is the slowest, taking almost thirty years to orbit the Earth, while the Moon is the fastest, orbiting in less than thirty days. This sequence, Saturn, Jupiter, Mars, Sun, Venus, Mercury, Moon, is called the Chaldean Order of the planets.

The planetary hours use the Chaldean order to divide time. Each planetary hour of the planetary day is ruled by a different planet. The planet that rules the first hour of the day is also the ruler of the whole day and gives the day its name. Thus the first hour of Sunday is ruled by the Sun, the first hour of Monday is ruled by the Moon and so on. This can be seen in the following two tables which are standard diagrams of the sequence of the planetary hours.

Planetary Hours of the Day

Hour	Sunday	Monday	Tuesday	Wednesday	Thursday	Friday	Saturday
1	Sun	Moon	Mars	Mercury	Jupiter	Venus	Saturn
2	Venus	Saturn	Sun	Moon	Mars	Mercury	Jupiter
3	Mercury	Jupiter	Venus	Saturn	Sun	Moon	Mars
4	Moon	Mars	Mercury	Jupiter	Venus	Saturn	Sun
5	Saturn	Sun	Moon	Mars	Mercury	Jupiter	Venus
6	Jupiter	Venus	Saturn	Sun	Moon	Mars	Mercury
7	Mars	Mercury	Jupiter	Venus	Saturn	Sun	Moon
8	Sun	Moon	Mars	Mercury	Jupiter	Venus	Saturn
9	Venus	Saturn	Sun	Moon	Mars	Mercury	Jupiter
10	Mercury	Jupiter	Venus	Saturn	Sun	Moon	Mars
11	Moon	Mars	Mercury	Jupiter	Venus	Saturn	Sun
12	Saturn	Sun	Moon	Mars	Mercury	Jupiter	Venus

Planetary Hours of the Night

Hours	Sunday	Monday	Tuesday	Wednesday	Thursday	Friday	Saturday
1	Jupiter	Venus	Saturn	Sun	Moon	Mars	Mercury
2	Mars	Mercury	Jupiter	Venus	Saturn	Sun	Moon
3	Sun	Moon	Mars	Mercury	Jupiter	Venus	Saturn
4	Venus	Saturn	Sun	Moon	Mars	Mercury	Jupiter
5	Mercury	Jupiter	Venus	Saturn	Sun	Moon	Mars
6	Moon	Mars	Mercury	Jupiter	Venus	Saturn	Sun
7	Saturn	Sun	Moon	Mars	Mercury	Jupiter	Venus
8	Jupiter	Venus	Saturn	Sun	Moon	Mars	Mercury
9	Mars	Mercury	Jupiter	Venus	Saturn	Sun	Moon
10	Sun	Moon	Mars	Mercury	Jupiter	Venus	Saturn
11	Venus	Saturn	Sun	Moon	Mars	Mercury	Jupiter
12	Mercury	Jupiter	Venus	Saturn	Sun	Moon	Mars

However, the planetary hours are not the same as the sixty minute hours beginning at midnight which we use for normal timekeeping. The planetary days are divided into twenty-four planetary hours with the first hour of the day beginning at sunrise and the last hour of the day ending at sunrise of the next planetary day. The period that extends from sunrise to sunset (daylight) is divided into twelve hours and the period extending from sunset to sunrise of the next day (nighttime) is also divided into twelve hours giving the twenty four hours of the planetary day.

Accordingly, as the duration of a day's daylight and darkness differ except at the time of the Vernal and Autumnal Equinoxes, on a particular planetary day the length of the hours of the day will differ from the length of the hours of the night. Thus another name for the planetary hours, says the English astrologer William Lilly, is the unequal hours.

As Lilly notes, there are seven days of the week and seven planets, and each planet rules or is lord of one day: Sunday, the Sun; Monday, the Moon; Tuesday, Mars; Wednesday, Mercury; Thursday, Jupiter; Friday, Venus; and Saturday, Saturn.[5] The origin of the names of the days are explicitly planetary in medieval Latin: *dies dominici* (Sunday, the Lord's day), *dies Lune* (Monday, Moon day), *dies Martis* (Tuesday, Mars day), *dies Mercuri* (Wednesday, Mercury day), *dies Jovis* (Thursday, Jupiter day), *dies Veneris* (Friday, Venus day), *dies Saturni* (Saturday, Saturn day). In English the Teutonic equivalents of the Greek and Latin gods have been used for some of the names of the days, i.e. Tuesday is Tiw's day, the Teutonic god of war; Wednesday is Wotan's day; Thursday is Thor's day; Friday is Frigg's day.

Note that the sequence and names of the days of the week are not in the Chaldean order, but nevertheless relate to it. Two processes interact to produce the sequence of the days of the week: (1) the fact that the planetary hours follow the Chaldean order; and (2) the fact that the planet

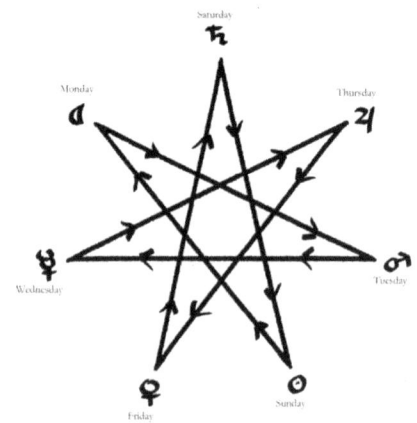

[5] William Lilly, *Christian Astrology*, page 482.

that rules the first hour of each day rules the whole day and gives the day its name.

To right is the standard diagram of the planets arranged in a circle in the Chaldean order. Starting with the Sun and then following the order of the days of the week and their planetary rulers, i.e. Moon, Mars, Mercury, Jupiter, Venus, Saturn, produces a seven pointed star, the heptagram of the week.

The sequence of the planetary hours in the Chaldean order and the rulership of the planetary day by the first planetary hour ruler produces the order and names of the days of the week. Thus we can see that the order and names of the days of the week are not merely conventional, but part of an ancient natural and highly ordered astrological system.

There are various types of software for determining the planetary hours, including my own TPHP planetary hours program which is provided free to students of my Planetary Magic Mini-Course and full Astrological Magic Course. However, it is useful to understand how to do the process by hand. The necessary sunrise and sunset times can be obtained from the U.S. Naval Observatory using your own location, or you can obtain your local sunrise and sunset times from the newspaper. Take the time from sunrise to sunset and convert it into seconds. There are 60 seconds in a minute and 60 minutes in an hour, so there are 3,600 seconds in an hour. Using seconds allows for precise fractions of an hour.

For example, if the Sun rises on Sunday at 6:00 am and sets at 6:24 pm, the length of the planetary day is 12 hours and 24 minutes. (12 x 60 = 720 minutes x 60 = 43,200 seconds) + (24 x 60 = 1440 seconds) = 44, 640 seconds. Don't worry if the time is not provided in seconds from your source, minutes are precise enough, and you can still do your calculations in seconds. Divide by twelve to get the length of each planetary hour for the day. 44, 460 divided by 12 equals 3720 seconds. This equals 1 hour, 2 minutes (3600 seconds divided by 60 = 60 minutes = 1 hour) 3720 - 3600 = 120 seconds (120 divided by 60 = 2 minutes).

So if we start at sunrise at 6:00, then the first planetary hour extends from 6:00 to 7:02 am. The second from 7:02 to 8:04 and so on. We repeat the same process for the period from sunset to the sunrise of the next day. Because of the rounding of the fractional second we won't be absolutely precisely on the mark, but a few seconds variation is acceptable.

Then starting with the planet that rules the day , e.g., the Sun for Sundays, follow the Chaldean order and assign the proper planet to each planetary hour of the day and night that you have just calculated. For example, if Sunrise on Sunday is at 6:00, then Sun hour starts at 6:00 am and ends at 7:02 am. At 7:02 am, Venus hour starts. At 8:04 am, Venus hour ends and Mercury hour begins. At 9:06 am, Mercury hour ends and Moon hour begins. At 10:08 am, Moon hour ends and Saturn hour, beginning the Chaldean order cycle, begins. The hours of the planetary day of the Sun thus continue through the Chaldean order for a total of 24 hours until dawn on Monday. Note that because the conventional day begins at Midnight, the planetary hour of the Sun continues into conventional Monday, lasting until Sunrise.

IV

PLANETARY HOUR ELECTIONS

T he planetary hours are a useful part of electional astrology, the branch of astrology which allows us to choose auspicious times to take action. Generally we would choose to take action during the planetary hour of the planet that rules the activity we wish to undertake. We can check our planetary rulership tables, found in the Appendices for guidance. For example, the medieval Arabic astrologer Al-Biruni says Mercury rules selling books, so if I wanted to send a book proposal to a publisher I could do it in the hour of Mercury.[6] For additional strength, take the action in the day as well as the hour of the chosen planet. We can also use the planetary days and hours to make planetary talismans, as will be explained later in detail.

In addition to this general advice regarding timing by planetary hours, the English astrologer, Henry Coley in his 1676 book, *Clavis Astrologiae Elimata* or, *A Key to the Whole Art of Astrology* gives the following detailed suggestions for using the planetary hours:

Here it will be necessary, briefly to shew the Signification of each Planetary Hour, and what use may be made of them, &c.

---

[6] See Appendix A.

In the hour of Saturn take no Voyage to Sea, neither take any long Journey by Land; for crosses will surely attend, and small success may be expected; take no Physick: entertain no Servant, for they will prove idle, careless Persons: Not good to put on a new Garment, or cut your Hair, but this hour is good to buy, or take Leases of Houses or Lands; good to buy any kind of Grain, or dig in the Earth or Plow; not good to borrow Money in this hour, or to fall sick in; for it threatens long Disease and sometimes terminates in death.

In the hour of Jupiter tis good to apply to Ecclesiastical Persons and all great Men to obtain their favour; the same from all grave Senators, Judges, Lawyers, &c. In this hour tis good to take a Journey; or to go out of the House with success; good to sow all kind of Seeds or to Plant; not good to be let blood; he that falls sick in this hour will soon recover; good also to lend, or borrow Moneys; not good to enter a Ship; not good to buy Beasts: to conclude this hour is good to Contract Matrimony in, &c.

In the hour of Mars begin no worthy Action, or Enter-prize, for it is very unfortunate hour in all things, and there-fore as much as may be to be avoided, it is ill to take a Journey for you shall be in danger of Thieves; very ill to take a Voyage to Sea, and generally in all things.

The hour of the Sun, is not to be chosen, as being generally infortunate, unless in makeing Application to great Persons, not good to begin a building, or put on new Garments, not good to enter into a mans own house, for discontent and brawling may then be expected to follow, this hour is good for a man to receive preferment in, not good to Court the Female Sex or lay down moneys upon any account, 'tis also very dangerous for any person to fall sick in.

In the hour of Venus 'tis good to court Women, or to begin a Journey, but not a Voyage, good to enter upon any Play, Sport or pastime; not good to be let blood in, go House with success, but not so good to return again in, good to take Physick in, but if a Man falls sick in that hour, the disease proceeds from some Venereal distemper, this hour is generally good to undertake any business relating to the Womens concerns, or any delightful Actions, not good to begin a new Garment, but singular good for marriage, and contracting in Matrimony, &c

The hour of Mercury is very good to Merchandize in, viz. Buy or sell, or to write Letters, or to good to send Messengers, to take Physick in, to send Children to School, to begin a Journey, to lend or or to brrow Moneys in, to put forth Apprentices, to begin any Building, but not good to Contract Marriage, or to Buy Houses or Lands, or to Re-enter your House being abroad, lest discontent or Brawling arise; nor good to take or hire a Servant, or to Redeem a Prisoner, but good to Plant or Graff-in, and finally to make Suit to great Persons.

The hour of the Moon is not accounted good to Buy Cattle in, especialy of the smaller Sort, nor to take Physick in, or begin any Building, not good to lend Money in, or to make new Cloaths;'tis good to Court the Female Sex in, or send Children to School, and in some cases to take a Journey, or to pursue an Enemy, and to conclude, you may make choice of this hour to leave your Native Country in, (if designed to Travil) but choose another hour when you return, not and are to re-enter your own Countrey again.[7]

We also have suggestions for use of the planetary hours from the *Key of Solomon*, a 16th century grimoire or book of magic in Appendix C. The instructions in the *Key of Solomon* will be particularly useful when we wish to elect talismans, because many of its elections are for timing magical rituals and talismans.

Coley, after listing the planetary hour elections above, then pronounces:

These Significations of the Planetary Hours are very Ancient, approved of by the Arabians, Hand confirmed by Haly and later Authors, and may be of good use, though they are not of that efficacy as well-grounded Elections, from an apt positure of the Heavens, which doth sympathize with the Nativity (if it be known) of which I shall treat in the next Section.[8]

Coley is therefore saying that while planetary hour and day elections are useful, they are not as precise, accurate or powerful as full chart elections. This is logical because we are only taking into consideration one astrological factor, while in full chart elections we will consider not only the planetary day and hour, but a wide variety of other factors as well.

---

[7] Henry Coley , *A Key to the Whole Art of Astrology*, Book 2, Section IV.
[8] Ibid.

There are several ways to directly work with the planetary day and hour cycle. We can chose to take action at appropriate times, using the planetary days and hours, as suggested above and in the appendices. Alternatively, we can watch the planetary hours and days for a week and to note how they correspond to events. Conflict and arguments, for example, will often be found to correspond with Mars hour, important communications with Mercury hour and times of love and friendship with Venus hour. My experience and the experience of my students who have done this exercise is that the planetary hours correspond roughly 60%-70% to the actual cycle of events. This fits with Coley's comments regarding the accuracy of planetary days and hour used by themselves.

Another consideration, and this truly is a secret of planetary hours, since it appears in no traditional source that I have seen, is that the planetary hour cycle is affected by the current Zodiacal state of the planet. What this means is that if Venus is currently afflicted, for example, in Aries or Scorpio, her detriments, or in Virgo, her fall, then the days and hours of Venus will be affected as well and thus not as efficacious for love, friendship and other Venusian activities compared to those times when Venus is not afflicted. I have had personal experience with this in regard to talismans. I once made a Jupiter talisman on Jupiter day (Thursday) and Jupiter hour. However, Jupiter was in detriment and retrograde and so the talisman caused me to lose money!

V

ADVANCED PLANETARY ELECTIONS

While the planetary days and hours are a good start in terms of finding an appropriate time for an planetary election, in order to find the most powerful election, we must use the more complex techniques of traditional (pre-1700) astrology. A complete explanation of these techniques is beyond the scope of this book, however, to give readers a taste of the precision of traditional astrology and assist more practiced traditional astrologers in making advanced planetary elections, here are the rules that I have culled from our traditional sources.[9]

What we seek to do is find a time when the planet is most powerful, realizing that all elections involve some trade off; we cannot expect to find a perfect election. The Renaissance mage Cornelius Agrippa says:

---

[9] Note that complete instructions for full chart planetary elections, along all of other types of astrological magic are provided in my full Astrological Magic Course. Full chart advanced planetary elections are also available through PMP, my Planetary Magic Program, free to students of my Planetary Magic Mini-Course & full Astrological Magic Course. Information is available on these courses and software at my web site www.renaissanceastrology.com

Now we shall have the Planets powerfull when they are ruling in a House, or in Exaltation or Triplicity, or term, or face without combustion of what is direct in the figure of the heavens, viz. when they are in Angles, especially of the rising, or Tenth, or in houses presently succeeding, or in their delights.[10]

Agrippa also notes that neither the planet nor the Moon, important in all elections, should be afflicted. While many talismans have specific electional requirements, we can start by looking at a basic recipe for benefic planetary talismans. I have determined this selection of factors from looking at a wide variety of traditional sources including Cornelius Agrippa's *Three Books of Occult Philosophy*, Marsilio Ficino's *Three Books on Life* and the premier grimoire of medieval and Renaissance astrological magic, the *Picatrix*, as well as considering my own experience in creating hundreds of talismans using traditional methods. The following selection of factors balances practicality with the myriad requirements sometimes listed in traditional sources. As noted, what follows is a general recipe for a electing a planetary talisman and often our traditional sources list special, individual requirements. Keep in mind that if there are specific requirements for the particular talisman, these take precedence over the basic method, though adding in additional positive factors is never a problem unless it prevents you from doing the election.

* The planet should be dignified, preferably by sign or exaltation.

* The planet should be rising , i.e., conjunct the Ascendant, or culminating i.e., conjunct the Midheaven.

* It should be the hour and preferably the day of the planet

In addition, the planet and the Moon must be unafflicted. In other words neither the planet nor the Moon must be:

* Combust, that is within 8.5 degrees of the Sun

---

[10] Cornelius Agrippa, *Three Books of Occult Philosophy*, Bk II, ch 3.

* Retrograde or significantly slower than its average speed

* In detriment or fall

* Making an applying opposition or square of any planet or an applying conjunction, opposition or square of Saturn or Mars

* Conjunct the South Node of the Moon or the malefic fixed star Algol which is at 26 Taurus.

The presence of any one of the afflictions listed above invalidates the talisman election in the basic method or with a particular election recipe. Many talisman elections in our traditional sources call only for the hour of the planet, so this is more important than the day, and even the day of the planet can be dispensed with if necessary. We can also make a good talisman with the planet dignified by triplicity, but a term or face talisman would be rather weak.

Let's take a look at an example election for a Sun talisman.

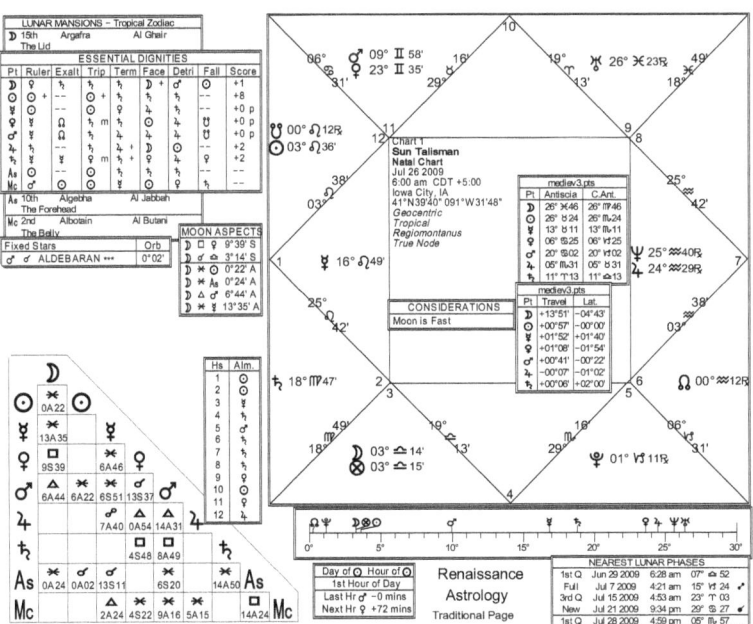

This election is for Iowa City, Iowa at 6:00 am CDT (Central Daylight Time) on July 26, 2009. The Sun is in his sign Leo, and as a bonus is dignified by triplicity as well, being the day ruler of fire signs in a fire sign by day. The Sun is rising because he is within 5 (we can stretch to 8) degrees of the Ascendant. Now with any other planet we could start at 5 degrees below the Ascendant and continue to 5 degrees above the Ascendant and consider the planet rising. However, we need to have the hour and if possible the day of the planet for the election, and planetary Sunday and Sun hour do not start until the Sun rises above the Ascendant.

Neither the Sun nor the Moon are making any applying negative aspects and in fact the Moon applies to a sextile of the Sun, which is very auspicious, and is conjunct the benefic Part of Fortune. The Moon is not otherwise afflicted.

Now having determined the start of the election, which is when all of the desired factors are first in operation, we need to look for a stop time. In this case the first factor to end is when the Sun moves more than five degrees from the Ascendant at 6:25 am, so this is our stop time.

For a planetary talisman we would thus want to complete the making the talisman during that time range. But it is fine to continue and complete the consecration ritual beyond the stopping time, if necessary, provided we began our ritual within the time frame.

This is just a surface overview of the complexity of full chart planetary elections. The necessary energy and effort to master their mysteries, however, is fully compensated by their power and precision.

VI

PLANETARY TALISMANS

The most basic form of astrological magic is planetary magic which uses the seven traditional planets. First the mage decides what effect to manifest. For example, suppose the mage desires eloquence and good memory. The mage then selects a planet that embodies the chosen Divine Idea or rules the desired effect. In this case, the  planet Mercury is appropriate, as he rules speech and communication. The mage then selects a time when Mercury is strong. As we have seen in full chart planetary elections there are many factors that must be considered when deciding whether a planet is strong, but we can make effective use of the planetary days and hours for timing a planetary talisman.

At the selected time, the mage creates a talisman from materials that are ruled by the chosen planet or star and so contain the essence of the selected Divine Idea. Mercury, for example, rules the gemstones agate, marcasite and topaz, the plants lungwort and marjoram, and mixed colors .[11] Though they are less powerful and long lasting, paper talismans can also be created by coloring in black and white talisman images.

Finally, when constructing the talisman, it is important to conduct certain rituals in order to consecrate and charge the talisman. Because each person, like the Cosmos, has a body, soul and Divine Spirit, we are closely and harmoniously connected to the Anima Mundi, the Soul of the World, a key magical link. By choosing incense, candles, music, clothing and surroundings appropriate to the

---

[11] William Lilly, *Christian Astrology*, see Appendix B.

planet, and calling upon and invoking the planet, we align ourselves with the planet and its embodied Divine Ideas, and so become a conduit for its energy. This further increases the power of the talisman. Each of the individual planetary pages lists the colors, incense and music of each planet which can be incorporated into the planetary ritual. You can even dress in appropriate planetary clothing as listed in Appendix D. Readers should keep in mind that the rituals provided in this book are suggestions and can be altered if desired. Ritual should appeal to you esthetically and stir your mind and senses. In addition, you can incorporate features from other magical systems, particularly if you already practice another system.

The first thing you need to do is set up an altar space. An altar can be quite elaborate or just a small space delineated by an appropriately colored cloth. I use the top of a bookshelf for my ritual work. The altar needs to be placed where you will be able to have some privacy and quiet during your ritual and where it will not be disturbed. Consult the planetary pages for an appropriate color for candles for the ritual. Black, for example, is the color of Saturn. White is a good neutral color and is suited for many kinds of benefic magic. Use white candles or even one white candle if you can't get candles in the appropriate planetary colors.

For an astrologically based choice for the number of candles, Cornelius Agrippa's *Three Books of Occult Philosophy*, Book II, chapter 22 notes the numbers corresponding to each planet. These numbers are provided on the planetary ritual later in this book. These numbers are also used for timing the number of days you repeat the invocation.

If you wish you can rub or anoint the candles with appropriate oils. The plants and herbs ruled by a planet, which you can find in the planetary rulership lists in Appendices A & B, give guidance for appropriate oils. You can even carve the candles with your name and goal using a needle or pin as well as add the various characters and symbols of the planets as shown on the planetary ritual pages. You can either do the anointing and carving of the candles at the beginning of your ritual work at the appropriate planetary hour or you can prepare the candles beforehand. Set the candles up in an appropriate pattern on your altar; a square for four or even number, a triangle for three or odd number, or a circle for a large number of candles. You can use candleholders or lightly melt the bottom of the candles and stick them on a plate. Be careful with candles! Do not let them burn unattended. If they fall over during your ritual this is a sign that the ritual is going to fail. Stop and try again at a later date.

You will also want to burn incense. Each planetary ritual lists the more easily available incense appropriate to the planet, though you can also use as incense the plants and herbs ruled by the planet, which are listed in Appendices A & B, or the planetary incense listed in Appendix D. You can use incense sticks or the actual raw incense. If you use raw incense you will need to burn it on special charcoal and you will also need an incense burner. Place it on a plate and be careful about touching the incense burner or leaving the charcoal burning unattended as it will get hot and is a definite fire hazard.

In preparation for your ritual have your altar space and materials ready and handy. For your paper talisman, have the black and white version of the planetary image ready. You can photocopy single copies of the planetary images from this book for personal use only. At the elected time, i.e., the appropriate planetary hour (and day if possible) prepare the candles or light the prepared candles and incense. Put on your planetary colored clothing, if desired. Color in the planetary image while meditating on it and add your name or the name of the person(s) you wish to affect and your goals.

Then invoke the planet, calling upon it. The various Hymns of Orpheus for invoking the planets are provided on the planetary ritual pages. The Renaissance sage Pico della Mirandola says, "Nothing is more effective in natural magic than the Orphic Hymns…"[12] While invoking the planet, move the colored talisman image back and forth through the smoke of the incense. This is know as suffumigation. Next meditate on the image of the planet as the emblem of its qualities and the embodiment of its virtues. Realize that the planet within you is connected to everything in the Material World with its qualities as well as the Celestial World and the Divine Ideas it incarnates. Then visualize the successful achievement of your goals. Do your best to let go of any worry or tension during this process; cultivate a calm confidence in the ritual and in your own magical powers.

For maximum power you should repeat this ritual of lighting incense and candles, invoking the planet, suffumigation, meditation and visualization for the appropriate number of days in a row, each time at the appropriate planetary hour. After you finish the multiple

---

[12] Pico della Mirandola, *900 Theses*, Section 10, thesis 1.

day ritual you can fold up the planetary image and carry it with you (in your wallet or purse is a good place) or keep it in the place where you wish the effect to manifest. Paper talismans seem to last about one to three months.

Ritual, along with astrological timing, is key to astrological magic. It is very valuable to do repeated ritual or to make planetary invocations on a regular basis. I do a daily planetary invocation to the planet ruling the day. By doing repeated or regular ritual you strengthen your affinity to the planets and the power of your talismans.

VII

PLANETARY RITUAL PAGES

A separate planetary ritual page is provided for each planet. Each page has complete ritual instructions listing suggested incense, colors for candles, altarcloth and clothing and appropriate numbers for each planet, used for picking the appropriate number of candles, and Orphic hymns to invoke each planet.

Also included is a beautiful black and white image for each planet by the noted contemporary esoteric artist and mage Nigel Jackson, who created the images from the descriptions provided in Cornelius Agrippa's *Three Books of Occult Philosophy* and *Picatrix*. Reader may make a single copy of an image for personal use when doing a planetary ritual.

These rituals are suggestions; readers should feel free to experiment and to add in ritual from the magical traditions in which they work.

SATVRN

RITUAL OF SATURN

(1) Preparations beforehand:

Get some candles and incense. Black candles are appropriate for Saturn. For incense, traditionally bad smelling incense was used for Saturn, but this doesn't appeal to me! I use pine. The numbers of Saturn are 3 or 9 according to Cornelius Agrippa.

Set up an altar. I use a piece of black cloth that is about 10" x 24."
Paper is fine, too. First set up the incense burner, then the candles
(in holders or melted a little on the bottom and stuck to a plate) and
have the Saturn image ready.

(2) On a Saturday (Saturn day) at dawn (Saturn hour)

(A) Light the candles and incense.

(B) Color in the Saturn talisman image adding your name or the
name of the person(s) you wish to affect and your goal.

(C) Move the Saturn talisman image back and forth through the
rising smoke of the incense and recite the Hymn to Saturn:

The Orphic Hymn to Saturn

ETHERIAL father, mighty Titan, hear,
Great fire of Gods and men, whom all revere:
Endu'd with various council, pure and strong,
To whom perfection and decrease belong.
Consum'd by thee all forms that hourly die,
Cronos as Lord of Time
By thee restor'd, their former place supply;
The world immense in everlasting chains,
Strong and ineffable thy pow'r contains
Father of vast eternity, divine,
O mighty Saturn, various speech is thine:
Blossom of earth and of the starry skies,
Husband of Rhea, and Prometheus wife.
Obstetric Nature, venerable root,

From which the various forms of being shoot;
No parts peculiar can thy pow'r enclose,
Diffus'd thro' all, from which the world arose,
O, best of beings, of a subtle mind,
Propitious hear to holy pray'rs inclin'd;
The sacred rites benevolent attend,
And grant a blameless life, a blessed end.

(E) Move the colored-in Saturn talisman back and forth through the smoke of the incense. Meditate on the Saturn talisman image. This is the embodiment of long life, stability, determination, discipline and deep and esoteric wisdom. Respectfully ask for Saturn's assistance. Meditate for about 10-15 minutes.

(3) Repeat the above ritual, starting on a Saturday (Saturn day) at Saturn hour for the next 2 or 8 days, for a total of 3 or 9 days. At dawn or at least in the morning repeat the lighting of the candles and incense, prayer, meditation and visualization. On the last day, let the candles burn all the way down, if possible. (No matter what the magical effect I never leave candles unattended).

(4) Place the colored-in talisman in the place where you wish to have the effects manifest.

JVPITER

RITUAL OF JUPITER

(1) Preparations beforehand:

Get some candles and incense. Gold, purple or yellow candles are nice for Jupiter, but white is fine, too. For incense, aloe wood (not the aloe vera that is used as a salve) is good, but any prosperity, good fortune or just pleasant smelling incense is fine. As for the number of candles, four is best but one white candle is okay.

Set up an altar. I use a piece of gold cloth that is about 10" x 24." You could use purple or yellow as well as gold. Paper is fine, too. First set up the incense burner, then the candles (in holders or melted a little on the bottom and stuck to a plate). Make a copy of the Jupiter talisman image.

(2) On a Thursday (Jupiter day) at dawn (Jupiter hour)

(A) Light the candles and incense.

(B) Color in the Jupiter talisman image adding your name or the name of the person(s) you wish to affect and your goal.

(C) Move the Jupiter talisman image back and forth through the rising smoke of the incense and recite the Hymn to Jupiter:

The Orphic Hymn to Jupiter

O Jove, much-honour'd, Jove supremely great,
To thee our holy rites we consecrate,
Our pray'rs and expiations, king divine,
For all things to produce with ease thro' mind is
thine.
Hence mother Earth and mountains swelling high
Proceed from thee, the deep and all within the sky.
Saturnian king, descending from above,
Magnanimous, commanding, sceptred Jove;
All-parent, principle and end of all,
Whose pow'r almighty shakes this earthly ball;
Ev'n Nature trembles at thy mighty nod,
Loud-sounding, arm'd with light'ning, thund'ring
God.
Source of abundance, purifying king,
O various-form'd, from whom all natures spring;
Propitious hear my pray'r, give blameless health,
With peace divine, and necessary wealth.

(E) Meditate on the Jupiter talisman image. This is the embodiment of wealth, prosperity, good fortune, justice, temperance and reason. Then visualize the achievement of your goal. Meditate for about 10-15 minutes.

(3) Repeat the above ritual at Jupiter hour for the next 3 days, for a total of 4 days.

(A) On the last day, let the candles burn all the way down, if possible. (No matter what the magical effect I never leave candles unattended).

(B) Place the talisman image where you wish the effect to manifest.

MARS

MARS RITUAL

(1) Preparations beforehand:

   Get some candles and incense. Red candles are best. For incense, use aloe wood, frankincense, dragon's blood, myrrh, or hot pepper (be careful not to get hot pepper smoke in your eyes). As for the number of candles, five is best but one red candle is okay.

   Set up an altar. I use a piece of red cloth that is about 10" x 24." Paper is fine, too. First set up the incense burner, then the candles (in holders or melted a little on the bottom and stuck to a plate) and have a copy of the Mars image available.

(2) On a Tuesday(Mars day) at dawn (Mars hour)

(A) Light the candles and incense.

(B) Color in the Mars talisman image adding your name or the name of the person(s) you wish to affect and your goal.

(C) Move the Mars talisman image back and forth through the rising smoke of the incense and recite the Hymn to Mars:

The Orphic Hymn to Mars

Magnanimous, unconquer'd, boistrous Mars,
In darts rejoicing, and in bloody wars
Mars as Lord of War
Fierce and untam'd, whose mighty pow'r can make
The strongest walls from their foundations shake:
Mortal destroying king, defil'd with gore,
Pleas'd with war's dreadful and tumultuous roar:
Thee, human blood, and swords, and spears
delight,
And the dire ruin of mad savage fight.
Stay, furious contests, and avenging strife,
Whose works with woe, embitter human life;
To lovely Venus, and to Bacchus yield,
To Ceres give the weapons of the field;
Encourage peace, to gentle works inclin'd,
And give abundance, with benignant mind.

(E) Meditate on the Mars talisman image. This is the embodiment of power, success, determination and achievement. Then visualize the achievement of your goal. Meditate for about 10-15 minutes.

(3) Repeat the above ritual at Mars hour for the next 4 for a total of 5 days.

(A) On the last day, let the candles burn all the way down, if possible. (No matter what the magical effect I never leave candles unattended).

(B) Put the Mars talisman image in the place where you wish the effect to manifest.

ThE SVN

SUN RITUAL

(1) Preparations beforehand:

Get some candles and incense. Gold, orange or yellow candles are nice, but white is fine. For incense, frankincense is good, but any prosperity, good fortune or just pleasant smelling incense is fine. Six is the number of the Sun, according to Agrippa, so use six candles, although one white candle is acceptable, too. Set up an altar. I use a piece of yellow cloth that is about 10" x 24" You could use orange or gold as well as yellow. Paper is fine, too. First set up the incense burner, then the candles (in holders or melted a little on the bottom and stuck to a plate) and have a copy of the Sun image available.

(2) At Sunday at Sunrise:

    (A) Light the candles and incense.

    (B) Color in the Sun talisman image adding your name or the name of the person(s) you wish to affect and your goal.

    (C) Move the finished Sun talisman image back and forth through the smoke of the incense and recite the hymn to the Sun. You can leave the image on the altar after each day's ritual.

TO THE SUN.

HEAR golden Titan, whose eternal eye
With broad survey, illumines all the sky.
Self-born, unwearied in diffusing light,
And to all eyes the mirrour of delight:
Lord of the seasons, with thy fiery car
And leaping coursers, beaming light from far:
With thy right hand the source of morning light,
And with thy left the father of the night.
Agile and vig'rous, venerable Sun,
Fiery and bright around the heav'ns you run.
Foe to the wicked, but the good man's guide,
O'er all his steps propitious you preside:
With various founding, golden lyre, 'tis mine
To fill the world with harmony divine.

Father of ages, guide of prosp'rous deeds,
The world's commander, borne by lucid steeds,
Immortal Jove, all-searching, bearing light,
Source of existence, pure and fiery bright
Bearer of fruit, almighty lord of years,
Agil and warm, whom ev'ry pow'r reveres.
Great eye of Nature and the starry skies,
Doom'd with immortal flames to set and rise
Dispensing justice, lover of the stream,
The world's great despot, and o'er all supreme.
Faithful defender, and the eye of right,
Of steeds the ruler, and of life the light:
With founding whip four fiery steeds you guide,
When in the car of day you glorious ride.
Propitious on these mystic labours shine,
And bless thy suppliants with a life divine.

(C) Meditate on the Sun talisman image. This is the embodiment of health, success and authority. Then visualize the achievement of your goal. Meditate for about 10-15 minutes.

(3) Repeat the above ritual for the next 5 days, for a total of 6 days, at Sun hour.

(A) On the last day, let the candles burn all the way down, if possible. (No matter what the magical effect I never leave candles unattended).

(B) Keep the talisman image in the place where you wish the effect to manifest.

VENVS

VENUS RITUAL

(1) Preparations beforehand:

Get some candles and incense. Red, pink or green candles are
nice, but white is fine. For incense, rose or musk is good, but any
love or just nice smelling incense is fine. Regarding the number of
candles, Agrippa says the number of Venus is 7. So 7 candles are
best but one white candle is fine. Set up an altar. I use a piece of
cloth that is about 10" x 24" You could use red, pink or green or
white cloth. Paper is fine, too. First set up the incense burner, then
the candles (in holders or melted a little on the bottom and stuck to a
plate) and the have the Venus talisman image available.

(2) At a Friday (Venus day) at Dawn (Venus hour)

(A) Light the candles and incense.

(B) Color in the Venus talisman image adding your name or the name of the person(s) you wish to affect and your goal.

(C) While moving the Venus talisman image through the rising smoke of the incense recite the Hymn to Venus:

The Orphic Hymn to Venus

Heav'nly, illustrious, laughter-loving queen,
Sea-born, night-loving, of an awful mien;
Crafty, from whom necessity first came,
Producing, nightly, all-connecting dame:
'Tis thine the world with harmony to join,
For all things spring from thee, O pow'r divine.
The triple Fates are rul'd by thy decree,
And all productions yield alike to thee:
Whate'er the heav'ns, encircling all contain,
Earth fruit-producing, and the stormy main,
Thy sway confesses, and obeys thy nod,
Awful attendant of the brumal God:
Goddess of marriage, charming to the sight,
Mother of Loves, whom banquetings delight;
Source of persuasion, secret, savoring queen,
Illustrious born, apparent and unseen:
Spousal, lupercal, and to men inclin'd,
Prolific, most-desir'd, life-giving, kind:
Great sceptre-bearer of the Gods, 'tis thine,

Mortals in necessary bands to join;
And ev'ry tribe of savage monsters dire
In magic chains to bind, thro' mad desire.
Come, Cyprus-born, and to my pray'r incline,
Whether exalted in the heav'ns you shine,
Or pleas'd in Syria's temple to preside,
Or o'er th' Egyptian plains thy car to guide,
Fashion'd of gold; and near its sacred flood,
Fertile and fam'd to fix thy blest abode;
Or if rejoicing in the azure shores,
Near where the sea with foaming billows roars,
The circling choirs of mortals, thy delight,
Or beauteous nymphs, with eyes cerulean bright,
Pleas'd by the dusty banks renown'd of old,
To drive thy rapid, two-yok'd car of gold;
Or if in Cyprus with thy mother fair,
Where married females praise thee ev'ry year,
And beauteous virgins in the chorus join,
Adonis pure to sing and thee divine;
Come, all-attractive to my pray'r inclin'd,
For thee, I call, with holy, reverent mind.

(E) Meditate on the Venus talisman image. This is the embodiment
of love, friendship and happiness. Visualize the achievement of your
goal. Meditate for about 10-15 minutes.

(3) For best effects repeat the above ritual at Venus for the next 6
days, for a total of 7.

(A) On the last day, let the candles burn all the way down, if possible. (No matter what the magical effect I never leave candles unattended).

(B) Put the Venus talisman image in the place where you wish the effect to manifest.

MERCVRY

MERCURY RITUAL

(1) Preparations beforehand:

Get some candles and incense. Mixed color candles are nice, but white is fine. For incense, cinnamon or frankincense is good, but any prosperity, good fortune or just pleasant smelling incense is fine. As far as how many candles, 8 is the number of Mercury according to Agrippa, but one white candle is fine, too.

Set up an altar. I use a piece of mixed color cloth that is about 10" x 24." Paper is fine, too. First set up the incense burner, then the candles (in holders or melted a little on the bottom and stuck to a plate) and have a copy of the Mercury talisman image available.

(2) At Wednesday (Mercury day) at dawn (Mercury hour):

(A) Light the candles and incense.

(B) Color in the Mercury talisman image adding your name or the name of the person(s) you wish to affect and your goal.

(C) Move the Mercury talisman image back and forth through the rising smoke of the incense and recite the hymn to Mercury.

The Orphic Hymn to Mercury

Hermes, draw near, and to my pray'r incline,
Angel of Jove, and Maia's son divine;
Prefect of contest, ruler of mankind,
With heart almighty, and a prudent mind.
Celestial messenger of various skill,
Whose pow'rful arts could watchful Argus kill.
With winged feet 'tis thine thro' air to course,
Emblems of Mercury
O friend of man, and prophet of discourse;
Great life-supporter, to rejoice is thine
In arts gymnastic, and in fraud divine.
With pow'r endu'd all language to explain,
Of care the loos'ner, and the source of gain.
Whose hand contains of blameless peace the rod,
Corucian, blessed, profitable God.
Of various speech, whose aid in works we find,
And in necessities to mortals kind.
Dire weapon of the tongue, which men revere,

Be present, Hermes, and thy suppliant hear;
Assist my works, conclude my life with peace,
Give graceful speech, and memory's increase.

(D) Meditate on the Mercury talisman image. This is the embodiment of wealth, thought, eloquence, business, speed, memory, trade, brokering and cunning. Then visualize the achievement of your goal. Meditate for about 10-15 minutes.

(3) Repeat the above ritual at Mercury hour for the next 7 days, for a total of 8.

(A) On the last day, let the candles burn all the way down, if possible. (No matter what the magical effect I never leave candles unattended).

     (B) Put the Mercury talisman image in the place where you wish the effect to manifest.

THE MOON

MOON RITUAL

(1) Preparations beforehand:

Get some candles and incense. White candles are appropriate. For incense, Agrippa says camphor and frankincense are lunar incenses. Nine is the number of the Moon, according to Agrippa, so use nine candles if you can or just one, as a practical alternative.

Set up an altar. I use a piece of white cloth that is about 10" x 24." First set up the incense burner, then the candles (in holders or melted a little on the bottom and stuck to a plate). Have a copy of the Moon talisman image available

(2) At Monday (Moon day) at dawn (Moon hour)

(A) Light the candles and incense.

(B) Color in the Moon talisman image adding your name or the name of the person(s) you wish to affect and your goal.

(C) Move the Moon talisman image back and forth through the rising smoke of the incense and recite the Hymn to the Moon:

The Orphic Hymn to the Moon

Hear, Goddess queen, diffusing silver light,
Bull-horn'd, and wand'ring thro' the gloom of
Night.
With stars surrounded, and with circuit wide
Diana, Goddess of the Moon
Night's torch extending, through the heav'ns you
ride:
Female and male, with silv'ry rays you shine,
And now full-orb'd, now tending to decline.
Mother of ages, fruit-producing Moon,
Whose amber orb makes Night's reflected noon:
Lover of horses, splendid queen of night,
All-seeing pow'r, bedeck'd with starry light,
Lover of vigilance, the foe of strife,
In peace rejoicing, and a prudent life:
Fair lamp of Night, its ornament and friend,
Who giv'st to Nature's works their destin'd end.
Queen of the stars, all-wise Diana, hail!
Deck'd with a graceful robe and ample veil.

Come, blessed Goddess, prudent, starry, bright,
Come, moony-lamp, with chaste and splendid
light,
Shine on these sacred rites with prosp'rous rays,
And pleas'd accept thy suppliants' mystic praise.

(D) Meditate on the Moon image. This is the embodiment of measured change, of the birth, life and death of all beings and all things. Knowledge of the secrets of the Moon brings success in travel and increase of psychic ability. Then visualize the achievement of your goal. Meditate for about 10-15 minutes.

(3) Repeat the above ritual at a Moon hour for the next 8 days, for a total of 9 days.

(A) On the last day, let the candles burn all the way down, if possible. (No matter what the magical effect I never leave candles unattended).

(B) Put the Moon talisman image in the place where you wish the effect to manifest.

APPENDIX A

AL-BIRVNI-S PLANETARY RVLERSHIPS

from Al-Biruni's *Book of Instruction in the Elements of the Art of Astrology*

ELEMENTAL QUALITIES, GENDER, TASTE & COLOR

Saturn is extremely cold and dry. The greater malefic. Male. Diurnal. Disagreeable and astringent, offensively acid, stinking. Jet-black also black mixed with yellow, lead color, pitch-dark.

Jupiter is moderately warm and moist. The greater benefic. Male. Diurnal. Sweet, bitter-sweet, delicious. Dust-color and white mixed with yellow and brown, shining, glittering.

Mars is extremely hot and dry. The lesser malefic. Male (some say female). Nocturnal. Bitter. Dark red.

The Sun is hot and dry, the heat predominant. Maleficent when near, beneficent at a distance.. Male. Diurnal. Penetrating, pungent, shining reddish-yellow, its color is said to be that of the lord of the hour.

Venus is moderately cold and moist, especially the latter. The lesser benefic. Female.- Nocturnal. Fat and sweet flavor. Pure white tending to straw-color, shining, according to some greenish.

Mercury is moderately cold and dry, the latter predominant. Beneficent. Male and diurnal by nature, but takes on the characters of others near. Complex flavor and color, the latter sky-blue mixed with a darker color.

The Moon is cold and moist, sometimes moderate, changeable. Beneficent and maleficent. Female. Nocturnal. Salt or insipid, somewhat bitter. Blue and white or some deep color not unmixed with reddish yellow, moderate brilliancy.

TEMPERATURE, QUALITIES, DAY, SOIL TYPE

Saturn: Coldest; hardest, most stinking and most powerful of things. Shortness, dryness, hardness, heaviness. Saturday (and Wednesday night) First climate. Barren mountains.

Jupiter: : Moderate, complete, pleasant, best and easiest things. Moderation, solidity, smoothness. Thursday (and Monday night). Second climate. Easily worked soil.

Mars: Hot, hard, sharp and red things. Length, dryness and coarseness. Tuesday (and Saturday night). Third climate. Waste, hard and stony land.

The Sun: Most expert, noble, well-known and generous things. Revolution, mines, worn-outness, empty and vacant places. Sunday (and Thursday night). Fourth climate. Mountains rich in minerals.

Venus: : Most pungent, most agreeable and delicious, most beautiful, softest and ripest things. Squareness, dispersion, smoothness. Friday (and Tuesday night). Firth climate. Soils with abundant water.

Mercury: Mixture of moderate things. Compounded of two things of this nature. Wednesday (and Sunday night) Sixth climate. Sandy soil.

The Moon: Thickest, densest, moistest and lightest objects. Density, moisture, opacity, lightness. Monday (and Friday night). Seventh climate. Plains and level ground.

RELIGIONS & PICTURES OF THE PLANETS

Saturn: Jews and those who dress in black. Old man seated on a wolf in his right hand the head of a man and in the left a man's hand; or according to another picture, mounted on a bright bay horse, on his head a helmet, in the left hand a shield and in the right a sword.

Jupiter: : Christians and those dressed in white. A young man with a drawn sword in the right hand and a bow and a rosary in the left, on horse-back; Another picture: man on a throne clad in variously colored robes, a rosary in the left hand.

Mars: Idolaters, wine-bibbers. dressed in red. Young man seated on two lions. in the right hand a drawn sword in the left a battle-axe; another picture: mounted on a bay horse, helmet on head, in the left hand a spear adorned with red roses, pennon flag, in the right hand head of a man, clad in red.

The Sun: Wearing a crown; Magians, Mithraists. A man seated on something like a shield on wheels drawn by. four oxen, in his right a staff on which he rests, in his left a mace, beads; another picture: man seated, face like a circle, holding reins of four horses.

Venus: : Islam. Woman on a camel holding a lute which she is playing; another picture: woman seated her hair unloosened the locks in her left hand, in the right a mirror in which she keeps looking. dressed in yellowish green, with a necklace, bells, bracelets and anklets.

Mercury: Disputants in all sects. Youth seated on a peacock, in his right hand a serpent and in the left a tablet which he keeps reading; another picture: man seated on a throne, in his hand a book which he is reading, crowned, yellow and green robe

The Moon: Adherents of the prevailing religion. Man with javelin in right hand. in his left thirty. you would think there were three hundred. on his head a crown, seated in a chariot drawn by four horses.

ACTIVITIES & MORALS

Saturn: Exile and poverty, or wealth acquired by his own trickery or that of others, failure in business, vehemence, confusion, seeking solitariness, enslaving people by violence or treachery, fraud, weeping and wailing and lamentation.

Jupiter: Friendliness, a peacemaker, charitable, devoted to religion and good works, responsible, uxorious, laughing, eloquent, eager for wealth, in addition to affability some levity and recklessness.

Mars: Marriage, travelling, litigation, business going to ruin, false testimony, lustful, a bad companion, solitary, spiteful and tricky.

The Sun: Longing for power and government, hankering after wealth and management of worldly affairs, and imposing will on the ignorant, reproving evil-doers, harsh with opponents. If Sun is in exaltation, the position is favorable to kings, if in fall to those in rebellion.

Venus: Lazy, laughing, jesting, dancing, fond of wine, chess, draughts, cheating, takes pleasure in every thing, not quarrelsome, a sodomite or given to excessive venery, well-spoken, fond of ornaments, perfume, song, gold, silver, fine clothes.

Mercury: Teaching manners, theology, revelation and logic, eloquent, fine voice, good memory for stories, ruining prospects by too great anxiety and misfortunes, fearful of enemies, frivolous, eager to buy slaves and girls, busybody , calumnious, thieving, lying and falsifying.

The Moon: Lying, calumniation, over-anxious for health and comfort, generous in distributing food, too uxorious, levity in appropriate places, excellent spirits.

MANNERS

Saturn: Fearful, timid, anxious, suspicious, miserly, a malevolent plotter, sullen and proud, melancholy, truth-te1ling, grave, trusty, unwi1ling to believe good of anyone, engrossed in his own affairs and consequently indicates discord, and either ignorance or intelligence, but the ignorance is concealed.

Jupiter: : Good disposition, inspiring, intelligent, patient, high-m1nded,devout, chaste, administering Justice, truth-te1ling, learned, generous, noble, cautious in friendship, egoistic, friend of good government, eager for education, an honorable trusty and responsible custodian, religious.

Mars: Confused opinions, ignorant, rash, evil conduct licentious, bold, quarrelsome, unsteady, untrustworthy, violent, shameless, unchaste but quickly repentant, a deceiver, cheerful, bright, friendly and pleasant-faced.

The Sun: Intelligent and knowledgeable, patient, chaste, but sensual, eager for knowledge, power and victory, seeking a good name for helping others, friendly, hot-tempered but quickly recovering repose.

Venus: : Good disposition, handsome face, good-natured inclined to love and sensuality, friendliness, generosity, tenderness to children and friends, pride, joy, patience.

Mercury: Sharp intelligence and understanding, affability, gentleness, open countenance, elegance, farsightedness, changeable, deeply interested in business, eager for pleasure, keeps secrets, seeking friendship of people, longing for power, reputation and approval, preserves true friends and withdraws from bad ones, keeps away from trickery, strife, malevolence, bad-heartedness and discord.

The Moon: Simple, adaptable, a king among kings, a servant among servants, good-hearted, forgetful, loquacious, timid, reveals secrets, a lover of elegance, respected by people, cheerful, a lover of women, too anxious, not intellectually strong, much thought and talk.

PROFESSIONS

Saturn: Building, paymaster, farming , reclaiming and distribution of water, fraudulent transactions, apportioning money and heritages, grave-digging; selling things made of iron, lead, bone, hair, copper, black slaves; knowledge used for bad purposes, such acts of the government as lead to evil oppression. wrath, captivity, torture.

Jupiter: : Noble actions, good government, religion, doing good; interpretation of dreams; goldsmiths work, banking; selling old gold and silver, white clothes, grapes and sugar-cane.

Mars: Law-making, selling and making armor, blacksmiths craft, grooms, shepherds, butchers. veterinary surgeons, surgeons, circumcisers, sellers of hounds, cheetahs, bears, wolves, copper, sickles, beer, glass, boxes, wooden cups, brigandage, contention, housebreaking, highwaymen, grave-robbers and prison, torture, execution.

The Sun: Receiving, giving and selling gold-brocades.

Venus: : Works of beauty and magnificence, fond of bazaars, commerce, measuring by weight, length and bulk; dealing in pictures and colors, goldsmiths work, tailoring, manufacturing perfumes, dealing in pearls, gold and silver ornaments, musk, white and green clothes, maker of crowns and diadems, accompanying singing, composing songs, playing the lute, feasts, games and gaming.

Mercury: Merchants, calculators and surveyors, astrologers. necromancers and fortune-tellers, geometrician, philosopher, disputation, poetry, eloquence, manual dexterity and anxiety for perfection in everything, selling slaves, hides, books, coins; profession of barbers, manufacture of combs.

The Moon: Engaged in business matters, missions. agencies, accounting; strenuous in religion and divine law, skill in all branches; practice of medicine, geometry, the higher sciences, measuring land and water; growing and cutting hair; selling food, silver rings and virgins. also indicates captivity, and prison for the deceptions of wizards.

RELATIVES & APPEARANCE

Saturn: Fathers, grandfathers, older brothers and slaves. Owners of estates, kings' intendants, religious or various sects, devotees, wicked people, bores, the overworked, eunuchs, thieves, the moribund, magicians, demons, ghouls, and those who revile them.

Jupiter: : Children and grandchildren. Kings, viziers, nobles, magnates, lawyers, merchants, the rich and their sycophants.

Mars: Brothers or middle age. Leaders, cavalry, troops, opponents, disputants in assembly.

The Sun: Fathers and brothers, slaves. Kings, nobles, chiefs, generals, officials, magistrates, physicians, societies.

Venus: : Wives, mothers, sisters, uterine kindred, delicate child. Nobles, Plutocrats, queens, courtesans, adulterers and their children.

Mercury: Younger brothers. Merchants, bankers, councilors, tax-collectors. slaves and wrestlers.

The Moon: Mothers, maternal aunts, elder sisters, nurses. Kings, nobles, noble matrons, celebrated, and wealthy citizens.

PARTS OF THE BODY

Saturn: Earth, black bile and occasionally crude phlegm. Hair, nails, skin, feathers, wool, bones, marrow and horn. Spleen.

Jupiter: Air and blood. Arteries, sperm and bone marrow. Heart in partnership with the Sun.

Mars: The upper part of fire and yellow bile. Veins and the hinder regions. Liver together with Venus.

The Sun: The lower part of fire. Brains, nerves, and the hypochondria, fat and everything of this kind. Stomaoh.

Venus: Flesh, fat and spinal marrow. Kidneys.

Mercury: Black bile. Arteries. Gall-bladder.

The Moon: phlegm, skin and everything related thereto Lungs.

MORE BODY PARTS

Saturn: Right ear. Hearing. Buttocks, podex, bowels, penis, back, height, knees. Old age.

Jupiter: : Left ear. Hearing and touch. Thighs and intestines, womb and throat. Middle age.

Mars: Right nostril. Smell and touch. pubes, gall-bladder, kidney. Youth.

The Sun: Right eye. Sight. Head and chest, sides, teeth, mouth. Full manhood.

Venus: : Left nostril. Smell and inhaling organs. Womb, genitals, hands and fingers. Youth and adolescence.

Mercury: Tongue together with Venus. Taste. Organs of speech. Childhood.

The Moon: Left eye. Vision and taste. Neck, breasts, lungs, stomach, spleen. Infancy to old age according to its various quarters.

DISEASES, APPEARANCE, RELATIVES

Saturn: Sickness, affliction, poverty, death, disease of internal organs, gout. Ugly, tall, wizened, sour face, large head, eyebrows joined, small eyes, wide mouth, thick lips; downcast look, much black hair, short neck, coarse hand, short fingers, awkward figure, legs crooked, big feet.

Jupiter: : Sickness, fatigue, fever, death in childbed, Caesarean section. Fine figure, round race, thick prominent, nose, large eyes, frank look, small beard, abundant curly hair reddish.

Mars: Fever. Brothers or middle age. Tall, large head, small eyes and ears, and fine forehead, sharp grey eyes, good nose, thin lips, lank hair, reddish, long fingers, long steps.

The Sun: Fathers and brothers, slaves. Large head, complexion white inclining to yellow, long hair, yellow in the white of the eye, stammers, large paunch with folds.

Venus: : Wives, mothers, sisters, uterine kindred, delicate child. Fine round face, reddish-white complex1on, double chin, fat cheeks, not too fat, fine eyes, the black larger than the white; small teeth, handsome neck, medium tall, short ringers, thick calves.

Mercury: Younger brothers. Fine figure, complexion brown with a greenish tinge, handsome, narrow forehead, th1ck ears, good nose, eyebrows joined, wide mouth, small teeth, thin beard, fine long hair, well-shaped long feet.

The Moon: Diseases of many kinds. Mothers, maternal aunts, elder sisters, nurses. Clear white complexion, gait and figure erect, round face, long beard, eyebrows joined, teeth separate crooked at the points, good hair with locks.

ANIMALS & BIRDS

Saturn: Black animals and those living in holes in the ground; oxen, goats, horses, sheep, ermine, sable, weasel , cat , mouse, jerboa, also black snakes, scorpions and other poisonous insects and fleas and beetles. Aquatic and nocturnal birds, ravens, swallows and flies.

Jupiter: Man, domestic animals and those with cloven hoots such as sheep, oxen, deer, those which are speckled and beautifully colored, and edible, or speaking, or trained such as lions, cheetahs and leopards. Birds with straight beaks , grain eating, not black, pigeon, francolin, peacock, domestic fowls, hoopoe and lark.

Mars: Lion, leopard, wolf, wild pig, dog, destructive or mad wild beasts, venomous serpents. Flesh-eating birds with curved bills , nocturnal, water hens, bats, all red birds, wasps.

The Sun: Sheep, mountain goat, deer, Arab horse, lion, crocodile, nocturnal anima1s which remain concealed during the day. Eagle, ring-dove, turtle dove, cock and falcon.

Venus: All those wild animals Which have white or yellow hoofs such as gazelle, wild ass, mountain goat also large fish. Ring-dove, wild pigeon, sparrow, bulbul, nightingale, locusts and inedible birds.

Mercury: Ass, camel, domestic dog, fox, hare, Jackal, ermine, nocturnal creatures, small aquatic and terrestrial animals. Pigeon, starling, crickets, falcon, aquatic birds and nightingales.

The Moon: Camel, ox, sheep, elephant, giraffe, all beasts of burden obedient to man and domesticated. Ducks, cranes, carrion crows, herons, chicks, partridge.

TREES & CROPS

Saturn: Oak-gall tree, citron or myrobalan tree. Olive tree and also willow, turpentine tree, castor-oil plant. and all those which bear fruits with disagreeable taste or smell, or hard-shells such as walnuts and almonds. Sesame.

Jupiter: : Trees bearing sweet fruit without hard skin such as peach, fig, apricot, pear and lote-fruit, companions Venus as to fruits. Roses, flowers. herbs sweet-smelling or tall, such plants as are light and whose seeds fly with the wind.

Mars: All bitter, pungent and thorny trees, their fruit with rough skin, pungent or very bitter such as bitter pomegranate, wild pear, bramble. Mustard, leeks, onion, garlic, rue, rocket, wild rue, radish, egg-plant.

The Sun: All tall trees which have oily fruit, and those whose fruit is used dry, such as date-palms, mulberries and vines. Dodder, sugar-cane. manna. tarangubin and shir-khisht.

Venus: : All trees soft to touch, sweet-smelling, smooth to the eye like cypress and teak. apple and quince. Sweet and oily berries. fragrant arid colored, herbs, spring flowers and has a share in cotton.

Mercury: pungent and evil-smelling trees. Savory herbs and garden stuff, canes and things growing in water.

The Moon: All trees the stem of which is short such as the vine and the sweet pomegranate. Grass. reeds, canes, flax, hemp, trailing plants such as cucumber and melon.

METALS, GEMS & FRUIT

Saturn: Litharge, iron slag, hard stones. Lead. Pepper, belleric myrobalan, olives, medlars, bitter pomegranate, lentils, liriseed, hempseed.

Jupiter: : Marcasite, tutty, sulfur, red arsenic, all white and yellow stones, stones found in ox-gall. Tin, white lead, fine-brass, diamond, all jewels worn by man. Wild pomegranate, apple, wheat, barley, rice, durra, chick peas, sesame.

Mars: Magnetic iron, shadna (lentil-shaped stones) cinnabar, rouge and mosaics (fasifusa). Iron and copper. Bitter almond, seed of turpentine-tree.

The Sun: : Jacinths, lapis lazuli, Yellow sulphur, orpiment, Pharaonic glass, marble, re-algar, pitch. Gold and whatever is coined therefrom for kings. Orange and maize.

Venus: : magnesia and antimony. Silver and gold and jewels set in these, household vessels made of gold, silver and brass, pearls, emeralds, shells. Figs, grapes, dates, origanum and fenugreek.

Mercury: Depilatory, arsenic, amber, all yellow and green stones. All coins struck with name and number such as dinars, dirhams and coppers, old gold and quicksilver, turquoise, coral, tree-coral. Peas, beans, caraway, coriander.

The Moon: Nabatean glass, white stones, emerald, moonstone. Silver and things manufactured of silver, such as cups, bangles, rings and the like, pearls, crystal, beads strung. Wheat, barley, large and small cucumbers, melons.

FOOD & DRUGS

Saturn: Drugs cold and dry in the fourth degree, especially those which are narcotic and poisonous. Dwellings. Sleep. Retentive power.

Jupiter: : Those which are moderately hot and moist and are profitable and agreeable. Fruits. Clothing. Vital, growing nutritive faculties and the air in the heart.

Mars: Whatever is not poisonous but pungent and warm in the fourth degree. Drugs. Business. Passion.

The Sun: Whatever is warm beyond the fourth degree and is salutary and in general use. Foods. Eating and drinking. Youthful vigor.

Venus: : Moderately cold and moist foods, useful and pleasant to the taste. Savory herbs. Coition. Sensuality.

Mercury: Foods which are dryer than cold and are agreeable but rarely useful. Grains. Speaking. Faculty of reflection.

The Moon: Foods which are equally cold and moist, sometimes useful, sometimes detrimental, and are not in constant use. Beverages. Drinking water. Natural power.

APPENDIX B

LILLY·S PLANETARY RVLERSHIPS

from William Lilly, *Christian Astrology*, (London, 1647) pages 57-83

Begin Page 57

Of the Planet SATURN, and his Signification.

NAMES He is called usually Saturn, but in some Authors Chronor, Phoenon, Falcifer.

COLOR He is the supreamest or highest of all Planets; is placed betwixt Jupiter and the Firmament, he is not very bright or glorious, or doth he twincle or sparkle, but is of a Pale, Wan or Leaden, Ashy colour slow in motion.

MOTION Finishing his Course through the twelve signs of the Zodiack in 29 yeers, 157 dayes, or thereabouts; his middle motion is two minutes and one second; his diurnall motion sometimes is three, four, five, or six minutes, or seldom more.

LATITUDE His greatest North Latitude from the Ecliptick is two degrees 48 minutes; his South Latitude from the Ecliptick is two degrees 49 minutes; and more then this he hath not.

HOUSES In the Zodiack he hath two of the twelve Signes for his Houses, viz. Capricorn his Night-house, Aquarius his Day-house; he has his Exaltation in Libra, he receives his Fall in Aries; he rejoyceth in the sign Aquarius.

TRIPLICITY, TERMS & FACE [Note Lilly does not use the standard Dorothean triplicity rulerships] He governeth the Aiery Triplicity by day, which is composed of these Signs; Gemini, Libra, Aquarius; [Terms] in all the twelve Signe he hath these degrees for his Terms, allotted him by Ptolemy.

In Aries, 27, 28, 29, 30.
In Taurus, 23, 24, 25, 26.
In Gemini, 22, 23, 24, 25.
In Cancer, 28, 29, 30.
In Leo, 1, 2, 3, 4, 5, 6.
In Virgo, 19, 20, 21, 22,23,24.
In Libra, 1, 2, 3, 4, 5, 6.
In Scorpio, 28, 29, 30.
In Sagittarius, 21, 22, 23, 24,25.
In Capricorn, 26, 27, 28, 29,30.
In Aquarius, 1, 2, 3, 4, 5, 6.
In Pisces, 27, 28, 29, 30.

The meaning whereof is, that if Saturn in any Question be in

Begin Page 58

any of these degrees wherein he hath a Term, he cannot be said to
be Peregrine, or void of essentiall dignities; or if he be in any of these
degrees allotted him for his Face or Decanate, he cannot then be said
to be peregrine: understand this in all the other Planets. He hath also
these for his Face or Decanate.

In Taurus, 21, 22, 23, 24, 25, 26, 27, 28, 29, 30.
In Leo, 1, 2, 3, 4, 5, 6, 7, 8, 9, 10.
In Libra, 11, 12, 13, 14, 15, 16, 17, 18, 19, 20.
In Sagittarius, 21, 22, 23, 24, 25, 26, 27, 28, 29, 30.
In Pisces, 1, 2, 3, 4, 5, 6, 7, 8, 9, 10.

He continueth Retrograde 140 dayes. He is five dayes in his first
station before Retrogradation,and so many in his second station
before Direction.

NATURE He is a Diurnall Planet, Cold and Dry (being far removed
from the heat of the Sun) and moyst Vapours, Melancholick, Earthly,
Masculine, the greater Infortune, author of Solitarinesse, Malevolent,
&c.

MANNERS & ACTIONS, WHEN WELL DIGNIFIED. Then he is
profound in Imagination, in his Acts severe, in words reserved, in

speaking and giving very spare, in labour patient, in arguing or disputing grave, in obtaining the goods of this life studious and solicitous, in all manner of actions austere.

WHEN ILL. Then he is envious, covetous, jealous and mistrustfull, timorus, sordid, outwardly dissembling, sluggish, suspicious, stubborn, a contemner of women, a close lyar, malicious, murmuring, never contented, ever repining.

CORPORATURE Most part his Body more cold and dry, of a middle stature; his complexion pale, swartish or muddy, his Eyes little and black, looking downward, a broad Forehead, black or sad Hair, and it hard or rugged, great Eares; hanging, lowring Eye-brows, thick Lips and Nose, a rare or thin Beard, a lumpish, unpleasant Countenance, either holding his Head forward or stooping, his Shoulders broad and large, and many times crooked, his Belly somewhat short and lank, his Thighs spare; lean and not long; his Knees and Feet indecent, many

Begin Page 59

times shoveling or hitting one against another, &c.

SATURN ORIENTALL You must observe, if Saturn be Orientall of the Sun, the stature is more short, but decent and well composed.

OCCIDENTALL The man is more black and lean, and fewer Hairs; and again, if he want latitude, the body is more lean, if he have great latitude, the body is more fat or fleshy; if the latitude be Meridionall or South, more fleshy; if the latitude be Meridionall or South, more fleshy, but quick in motion. If the latitude be North, hairy and much flesh. Saturn in his first station, a little fat. In his second station, fat, ill favoured Bodies, and weak; and this observe constantly in all the other Planets.

QUALITY OF MEN. In generall he signifieth Husbandmen, Clowns, Beggars, Day-labourers, Old-men, Fathers, Grand-fathers, Monks, Jesuits, Sectarists.

PROFESSION. Curriers, Night-farmers, Miners under ground, Tinners, Potters, Broom-men, Plummers, Brick-makers, Malsters, Chimney-sweepers, Sextons of Churches, Bearers of dead corps, Scavengers, Hostlers, Colliers, Carters, Gardiners, Ditchers, Chandlers, Diers of Black cloth, an Herdsman, Shepheard or Cow-keeper.

SICKNESSES. All Impediments in the right Ears, Teeth, all quartan Agues proceeding of cold, , dry and melancholly Distempers, Leprocies, Rheumes, Consumptions, black Jaundies, Palsies, Tremblings, vain Feares, Fantasies, Dropsie, the Hand and Foot-gout, Apoplexies, Dog-hunger, too much flux of the Hemoroids, Ruptures if in Scorpio or Leo, in any ill aspect with Venus.

SAVOURS. Sower, Bitter, Sharp, in mans body he principally ruleth the Spleen.

HEARBS. He governeth Beirsfoot, Starwort, Woolf-bane, Hemlock, Ferne, Hellebor the white and black, Henbane, Ceterach or Finger-ferne, Clotbur or Burdock, Parsnip, Dragon, Pulse, Vervine, Mandrake, Poppy, Mosse, Nightshade, Bythwind, Angelida, Sage, Box, Tutfan, Orage or golden Hearb, Spinach, Shepheards Purse, Cummin, Horitaile, Fumitory.

PLANTS and TREES. Tamarisk, Savine, Sene, Capers, Rue or Hearbgrice, Polipody, Willow or Sallow Tree, Yew-tree, Cypress tree, Hemp, Pine-tree.

Begin Page 60

BEASTS, &:c. The Asse, Cat Hare, Mouse, Mole, Elephant, Beare,,Dog, Wolf, Bastlisk, Crocodile, Scoprion, Toad, Serpent, Adder, Hog, all manner of creeping Creatures breeding of putrification, either in the Earth, Water or Ruines of Houses.

FISHES, BIRDS, &c. The Eele, Tortoise, Shel-fishes. The Bat or Blude-black, Crow, Lapwing, Owle, Gnat, Crane, Peacock, Grashopper, Thrush, Blackbird, Ostritch, Cuckoo.

PLACES. He delights in Deserts, Woods, obscure Vallies, Caves, Dens, Holes, Mountaines, or where men have been buried, Church-yards, &c. Ruinous Buildings, Cole-mines, Sinks, Dirty or Stinking Muddy Places, Wells and Houses of Offices, &c.

MINERALS. He ruleth over Lead, the Lead-stone, the Drosse of all Mettals, as also , the Dust and Rubbidge of every thing.

STONES. Saphire, Lapis Lazuli, all black, ugly Country Stones not polishable, and of a sad ashy or black colour.

WEATHER. He causeth Cloudy, Dark, obscure Ayre, cold and hurtfull, thick, black and cadense Clouds: but of this more particularly in a Treatise by it self.

WINDS. He delighteth in the East quarter of Heaven, and causeth Eastern Winds, at the time of gathering any Planet belonging to him, the Ancients did observe to turn their faces towards the East in his hour, and he, if possible, in an Angle, either in the Ascendant, or tenth, or eleventh house, the Moon applying by a Trine or Sextile to him.

ORBE. His Orbe is nine degrees before and after; that is,his influence begins to work, when either he applies, or any Planet applies to him, and is within nine degrees of his aspect, and from that aspect.

YEERS. In Generation he ruleth the first and eighth moneth after Conception.

The greatest yeers he signifies ---- 465.
His greater ---- 57.
His mean yeers ---- 43 and a half.
His least ---- 30.

Begin Page 61

The meaning whereof is this; Admit we frame a new building, erect a Town or City, or Family, or principality is begun when Saturn is essentially and accidentally strong, the Astrologer may probably conjecture the Family, Principality, &c. may continue 465 yeers in honour &c. without any sensible alteration: Again, if in ones Nativity Saturn is well dignified, is Lord of the Geniture, &c. then according to nature he may live 57 yeers; if he be meanly distinguished, then the Native but 43; if he be Lord of the Nativity, and yet weak, the child may live 30 yeers, hardly any more; for nature of Saturn is cold and dry, and those qualities are destructive to man, &c.

As to Age, he relates to decreped old men; Fathers, Grandfathers, the like in Plants, Trees, and all living Creatures.

COUNTRIES. Late Authours say he ruleth over Bavaria, Saxony, Stiria, Romandisle, Ravenna, Constantia, Ingoldstad.

ANGEL. Its Cassiel, alias Captiel.

His friends are Jupiter, Sun and Mercury, his enemies Mars and Venus. We call Saturday his day, for then he begins to rule at Sun rise, and ruleth the first hour and eighth of that day.

Of the Planet Jupiter, and his Signification.

Jupiter is placed next to Saturn (amongst the Ancients) you shall sometimes finde him called Zeus, or Phaeton: He is the greatest in appearance to our eyes of all the Planets (the Sun, Moon and Venus excepted;)

COLOR & MOTION In his Colour he is bright, cleer, and of an Azure colour. In his Motion he exceeds Saturn, finishing his course through the twelve Signes in twelve yeers: his middle motion is 4 min. 59 seconds: his Diurnal motion is 8,10,12 or 14 min. hardly any more.

LATITUDE His greatest North Latitude is ---- 1 38 His greatest South Latitude is ---- 1 40

HOUSES He hath two of the twelve Signe of the Zodiack for his houses, viz. Sagittarius his Day-house, and Pisces his Night-house.

Begin Page 62

He receives Detriment in Gemini and Virgo. He is Exalted in Cancer, hath his Fall in Capricorn.

TRIPLICITY, TERM & FACE [Note Lilly does not use the standard Dorothean triplicity rulerships] He ruleth the Fiery Triplicity by night, viz. Aries, Leo, Sagattarius. He hath also these degrees allotted for his Tearmes, viz.

Jupiter
In Aries, 1, 2, 3, 4, 5, 6
In Taurus, 16, 17, 18, 19, 20, 21, 22.
In Gemini, 8, 9, 10, 11, 12, 13, 14.
In Cancer, 7, 8, 9, 10, 11, 12, 13.
In Leo, 20, 21, 22, 23, 24, 25.
In Virgo, 14, 15, 16, 17, 18.
In Libra, 12, 13, 14, 15, 16, 17, 18, 19.
In Scorpio, 7, 8, 9, 10, 11, 12, 13, 14.
In Sagittarius, 1, 2, 3, 4, 5, 6, 7, 8.
In Capricorn, 13, 14, 15, 16, 17, 18, 19.
In Aquarius, 21, 22, 23, 24, 25.
In Pisces, 9, 10, 11, 12, 13, 14.

He hath assigned him for his Face or Decanate,

Of Gemini, 1, 2, 3, 4, 5, 6, 7, 8, 9, 10.
Of Leo, 11, 12, 13, 14, 15, 16, 17, 18, 19, 20.
Of Libra, 21, 22, 23, 24, 25, 26, 27, 28, 29, 30.
Of Capricorn, 1, 2, 3, 4, 5, 6, 7, 8, 9, 10.
Of Pisces, 11, 12, 13, 14, 15, 16, 17, 18, 19, 20.

He is Retrograde about 120 dayes, is five days in his first station before retrogradation, and four dayes stationary before Direction.

NATURE He is a Diurnall, Masculine Planet, Temperately Hot and Moyst, Aiery, Sanguine, the greater Fortune, author of Temperance, Modesty, Sobriety, Justice.

MANNERS & ACTIONS WHEN WELL DIGNIFIED.Then is he Magnanimous, Faithfull, Bashfull, Aspiring in an honourable way at high matters, in all his actions a Lover of fair Dealing, desiring to benefit all men, doing Glorious things, Honourable and Religious, of sweet and affable Conversation, wonderfully indulgent to his Wife and Children, reverencing Aged men, a great Reliever of the Poor, full of Charity and Godlinesse, Liberal, hating all Sordid actions, Just, Wife, Prudent, Thankfull, Vertuous: so that when you

Begin Page 63

find Jupiter the significator of any man in a Question, or Lord of his Ascendant in a Nativity, and well dignified, you may judge him qualified as abovesaid.

WHEN ILL When Jupiter is unfortunate, then he wastes his Patrimony, suffers every one to cozen him, is Hypocritically Religious, Tenacious, and stiffe in maintaining false Tenents in Religion; he is Ignorant, Carelesse, nothing Delightfull in the love of his Friends; of a grosse, dull Capacity, Schismaticall, abating himself in all Companies, crooching and stooping where no necessity is.

CORPORATURE He signifies an upright, straight and tall Stature; brown, ruddy and lovely Complexion; of an ovall or long Visage, and it full and fleshy; high Forehead; large gray Eyes; his Hair soft, and a kind of aburn brown; much Beard; a large, deep Belly: Strong proportioned Thighs and Legs; his feet long, being the most indecent parts of his whole Body; in his Speech he is Sober, and of grave Discourse.

ORIENTALL The skin more cleer, his complexion Honey-colour, or betwixt a white and red, sanguine, ruddy Colour; great Eyes, the body more fleshy, usually some Mole or Scarre in the right Foot.

OCCIDENTALL A pure and lovely Complexion, the Stature more short, the Hair a light Brown, or neer a dark Flaxen; smooth, bald about the Temple or Forehead.

QUALITY OF MEN. He signifies Judges, Senators, Councellours, Ecclesiasticall men, Bishops, Priests, Ministers, Cardinals,

Chancellours, Doctors of the Civill Law, young Schollers and Students in an University or College, Lawyers. Clothiers, Wollen-Drapers.

SICKNESSES. Plurisies, all Infirmities in the Liver, left Eare, Apoplexies, Inflamation of the Lungs, Palpitations and Trembling of the Heart, Cramps, pain in the Back-bone, all Diseases lying in the Vaines or Ribs, and proceeding from corruption of Blood, Squinzies, Windinesse, all Putrification in the Blood, or Feavers proceeding from too great abundance thereof.

SAVOURS. He governeth the Sweet or well sented odours; or that Odour which in smell is no way extream or offensive.

COLOURS Sea-green or Blew, Purple, Ash-colour, a mixt Yellow and Green.

Begin Page 64

HEARBS. Cloves and Clove-sugar, Mace, Nutmeg, Gilly- flower, the Straw-bury, the herb Balsam, Bettony, Centory, Flax, Ars-smart, Fumitory, Lung-wort, Pimpernel, Walwort, Orangy or Wild Margorane, Rubbarb, Self-heale, Borage, Buglosse, Wheat, Willow-hearb, Thorough-Leafe, Violets, Laskwort, Liverwort, Bazil, Pomergranets, Pyony, Liquorish, Mynt, Mastix, the dazy, Feversend, Saffron.

PLANTS and TREES. Cherry-tree, Birch-tree, Mulberry-tree, Corall-tree, the Oae, Barburies, Olive, Gooseburies, Almond-tree, the Ivy, Manna, Mace, the Vine, the Fig-tree, the Ash, the Pear-tree, the Hazel, the Beech-tree, the Pyne, Raysons.

BEASTS, &:c.The Sheep, the Heart or Stag, the Doe, the Oxe, Elephant, Dragon, Tyger, Unicorne, those Beasts which are Mild and Gentle, and yet of great benefit to Mankind, are appropriate to him.

BIRDS, &c. The Stork, the Snipe, the Lark, the Eagle, the Stock-dove, the Partridge, Bees, Pheasant, Peacock, the Hen.

FISHES. The Dolphin, the Whale, Serpent, Sheath-fish or River Whale.

PLACES. He delighteth in or neer Alters of Churches, in publick Conventions, Synods, Convocations, in Places neat, sweet, in Wardrobes, Courts of Justice, Oratorie.

MINERALS. & STONES. Tyn, Amethist, the Saphire, the Smarage or Emrald, Hyacinth, Topaz, Chrystal, Bezoar, Marble, and that which in England we call Free-stone.

WEATHER.He usually produceth serentiy, pleasant and healthful North Winds, and by his gentle Beams all ayes the ill weather of any former Malignant Planets.

WINDS. He governeth the North Wind, that part which tendeth to the East.

ORBE. His Radiation or Orbe, is nine degrees before and after any of his aspect.

GENERATION. He governeth the second and tenth moneth; his proper seat in man is the Liver; and in the Elements he ruleth the Ayre.

YEERS. His greatest yeers are 428. his greater 79. his mean 45. least 12.

AGE. Men of middle age, or of a full Judgment and Discretion.

Begin Page 65

CLIMATE. He governeth the second Climate.

COUNTRIES. Babylon, Persia, Hungaria, Spain, Cullen.

NUMBER. The number of three is attributed to him.

ANGEL. Zadkiel.

DAY OF THE WEEK. Thursday, and rules the first hour after Sun rise, and the eighth; the length of the Planetary hour you must know by the rising of the Sun, and a Table hereafter following.

All Planets except Mars are friends to Jupiter. In gathering any Hearb appropraited to Jupiter, see that he be very powerfull either in Essential or Accidental Dignities, and the Moon in some manner in good aspect with him, and if possible, let her be in some of his Dignities, &c.

Of the Planet MARS, and his Signification.

MARS doth in order succeed Jupiter, whom the Ancients sometimes called Mavors, Aris, Pyrois, Gradivus;

COLORS & LATITUDE He is lesse in body then Jupiter or Venus, and appeareth to our sight of a shining, fiery, sparkling colour, he finisheth his course in the Zodiack in one yeer 321 dayes, or thereabouts; his greatest latitude North is 4, 31 min. his South is 6 degr. and 47.

MOTION His mean motion is 31 min. 27 seconds. His diurnall motion is sometimes 32. 34. 36. 38. 40. 44. min. a day, seldom more.

HOUSES He hath Aries for his Day-house, and Scorpio for his Night-house; he is exalted in 28 degr. of Capricorn, and is depressed in 28 Cancer, he receiveth detriment in Libra and Taurus; he is retrograde 80 dayes; stationary before direction two dayes; after, but one day.

TRIPLICITY, TERMS AND FACE [Note Lilly does not use the standard Dorothean triplicity rulerships] He governeth wholly the Watry Triplicity, viz. Cancer, Scorpio, Pisces. In the whole twelve Signs, Ptolomy assigneth him these degrees for Terms, viz.

Begin Page 66

In ARIES, 22, 23, 24, 25,26.
In TAURUS, 27, 28, 29, 30.

In GEMINI, 26, 27, 28, 29,30.
In CANCER, 1, 2, 3, 4, 5, 6.
In LEO, 26, 27, 28, 29,30.
In VIRGO, 25, 26, 27, 28, 29, 30.
In LIBRA, 25, 26, 27, 28, 29, 30.
In SCORPIO, 1, 2, 3, 4, 5, 6.
In SAGITTARIUS, 26, 27, 28, 29, 30.
In CAPRICORN, 20, 21, 22, 23, 24, 25. In AQUARIUS, 26, 27, 28, 29, 30.
In PISCES, 21, 22, 23, 24, 25, 26.

He hath allotted him for his Face these degrees.

In ARIES, 1, 2, 31 4, 5, 6, 7, 8, 9, 10.
In GEMINI, 11, 12, 13, 14, 15, 16, 17, 18, 19, 20.
In LEO, 21, 22, 23, 24, 25, 26, 27, 28, 29, 30.
In SCORPIO, 1, 2, 3, 4, 5, 6, 7, 8, 9, 10.
In CAPRICORN, 11, 12, 13, 14, 15, 16, 17, 18, 19, 20.
In PISCES, 21, 22, 23, 24, 25, 26, 27, 28, 29, 30.

NATURE He is Masculine, Nocturnall Planet, in nature hot and dry, cholerick and fiery, the lesser Infortune, author of Quarrels, Strifes, Contentions.

MANNERS & ACTIONS WHEN WELL DIGNIFIED In feats of Warre and Courage invincible, scourning any should exceed him, subject to no Reason, Bold, Confident, Immoveable, Contentious, challenging all Honour to themselves, Valiant, lovers of Warre and things pertaining thereunto, hazarding himself to all Perils, willingly will obey no body; nor submit to any, a large reporter of his own Acts, one that fights all things in comparison of Victory, and yet of prudent behaviour in his own affaires.

WHEN ILL Then he is Pratler without modesty or honesty, a lover of Slaughter and Quarrels, Murder, Theevery, a promoter of Sedition, Frayes and Commotions; and Highway-Theef, as wavering as the Wind, a Traytor, of turbulent Spirit, Perjurer, Obscene, Rash, Inhumane, neither fearing God or caring for man, Unthankful, Trecherous, Oppressors, Ravenous, Cheater, Furious, Violent.

Begin Page 67

CORPORATURE Generally Martialuts have this forme; they are but middle Stature, their Bodies strong, and their Bones big, rather leane then fat; their Complexion of a brown, ruddy colour, or flaxen, and many times crisping or curling, sharp hazle Eyes, and they piercing, a bold confident countence, and the man active and fearlesse.

ORIENTALL When Mars is Orientall, he signifies Valiant men, some white mixed with the rednesse, a decent talnesse of Body, hairy of his Body.

OCCIDENTALL Very ruddy Complexion'd, but mean in Stature, little Head, a smooth Body, and not hairy; yellow Hair, stiffe, the natural humours generally more dry.

PRINCES. Ruling by Tyranny and Opression, or Tyrants, Usurpers, new Conquerours.

QUALITY OF MEN & PROFESSION. Generals of Armies, Colonels, Captaines, or any Souldiers having command in Armies, all manner of Souldiers, Physitians, Apothecaries, Chirurgions, Alchimists, Gunners, Butchers, Marshals, Sergeants, Bailiffs, Hangmen, Theeves, Smiths, Bakers, Armourers, Watch-makers, Botchers, Tailors, Cutlers of Swords and Knives, Barbers, Dyers, Cooks, Carpenters, Gamesters, Bear-wards, Tanners, Carriers.

SICKNESSES. The Gall, the left Eare, tertian Feavers, pestilent burning Feavers, Megrams in the Head, Carbunckles, the Plague and all Plague-sores, Burnings, Ring-wormes, Blisters Phrensies, mad sudden distempers in the Head, Yellow-jaundies, Bloody-flux, Fistulaes, all Wounds and Diseases in mens Genitories, the Stone both in the Reins and Bladder, Scars or smal Pocks in the Face, all hurts by Iron, the Shingles, and such other Diseases as arise by abundance of too much Choller, Anger or Passion.

COLOURS & SAVOURS. He delighteth in Red colour, or yellow, fiery and shinning like Saffron; and in those Savours which are bitter, sharp and burn the Tongue; of Humours, Choller.

HEARBS. The Hearbs which we attribute to Mars are such as come near to a rednesse, whose leaves are pointed and sharp, whose taste is costick and burning, love to grow on dry places, are corosive and penetrating the Flesh and Bones with a most subtil heat: They are as followeth. The Nettle, all manner of

Begin Page 68

Thistles, Rest-harrow or Cammock, Devils-milk or Petty spurge, the white and red Brambles, the white called vulgarly by the Hearbalists Ramme, Lingwort, Onion, Scommony, Garlick, Mustard-seed, Pepper, Ginger, Leeks, Ditander, Hore-hound, Hemlock, red Sanders, Tamarindes, all Hearbs attracting or drawing choller by Sympathy, Raddish, Castoreum, Arsolarr,Assarum, Carduus, Denedictus, Cantharides.

TREES. All Trees which are prickly, as the Thorn, Chestnut.

BEASTS, &:c. Panther, Tyger, Mastiffe, Vulture, Fox; of living creatures, those that are Warlike, Ravenous and Bold, the Castor, Horse, Mule, Ostrich, the Goat, the Wolf, the Leopard, the wild Asse, the Gnats, Flyes, Lapwing, Cockarrice, the Griffon, Bear.

FISHES, BIRDS, &c. The Pike, the Shark. the Barbel, the Fork-fish, all stinking Worms, Scorpions.

BIRDS. The Hawke, the Vultur, the Kite or Glead, (all ravenous Fowle) the Raven, Cormorant, the owle, (some say the Eagle) the Crow, the Pye.

PLACES. Smiths, Shops, Furnaces, Slaughter-houses, places where Bricks or Charcoales are burned, or have been burnes, Chimneys, Forges.

MINERALS.Iron, Antimony, Arsenick, Brimston, Ocre.

STONES. Adamant, Loadstone, Blood-stone, Jasper, the many coloured Amatheist, the Touch-stone, red Lead or Vermilion.

WEATHER. Red Clouds, Thunder, Lightning, Fiery impressions, and pestilent Airs, which usually appear after a long time of drinesse and fair Wheather, by improper and unwholesome Mysts.
WINDS. He stirreth up the Western Winds.

ORBE. His Orbe is onely seven degrees before and after any of his aspects.

YEERS. In man he governeth the flourishing time of Youth, and from 41 to 56; his greatest yeers are 264, greater 66, mean 40, lesse 15.

COUNTRIES. Saromatia, Lumbardy, Batavia, Ferraria, Gothland, and the third Climate.

DAY OF THE WEEK. He governeth Tuesday, and therein the first hour and eighth from Sun rise, and in Conception the third moneth.

ANGEL. Samael. His friends are onely Venus; Enemies all the other Planets.

Begin Page 69

Of the the SUN, his generall and particular Significations.

SOL The Sun is placed in the middle of all Planets, and is called amongst the Ancients, both Poets and Historians, Sol, Titan, Ilioa, Phebus, Apollo, Pean, Osyris, Diespiter:

It's needlesse to mention his Colour, being so continuallly visible to all mortal men: He passeth through all the twelve Signs of the Zodiack in one yeer, or 365 dayes and certain hours:

MOTION His mean motion is 59 min. 8 seconds, yet his diurnal motion is sometimes 57m 16 seconds, sometimes more, never exceeding 61 minutes and six seconds. He always moves in the Ecliptick, and is ever voyd of latitude, so that it is very improper in any Astrologian to speak of the Sun his latitude.

HOUSE He hath onely the Sign of Leo for his House, and Aquarius for his Detriment. He is Exalted in the 19 degree of Aries, and receives his Fal in 19 Libra.

TRIPLICITY [Note Lilly does not use the standard Dorothean triplicity rulerships] The Sun governeth the fiery Triplicity, viz. Aries, Leo, Sagittarius by day.

TERMS He hath no degrees of the twelve Signes admitted him for his Terms, though some affirm, if he be in the six Northern Signs, viz. Aries, Taurus, Gemini, Cancer, Leo, Virgo, he shal be said to be in his Terms, but because there is no reason for it, I leave it as Idle.

In the twelve Signs he hath these degrees for his Decanate or Faces.

In ARIES, the 11, 12, 13, 14, 15, 16, 17, 18, 19, 20.
In GEMINI, the 21, 22, 23, 24, 25, 26, 27, 28, 29, 30.
In VIRGO, the 1, 2, 3, 4, 5, 6, 7, 8, 9, 10.
In SCORPIO, the 11, 12, 13, 14, 15, 16, 17, 18, 19, 20.
In CAPRICORN, the 21, 22, 23, 24, 25, 26, 27, 28, 29, 30.

The Sun is alwayes direct, and never can be said to be Retrograde, it's true, he moveth more slowly at one time then another.

Begin Page 70

NATURE He is naturally Hot, Dry, but more temperate then Mars; is a Masculine, Diurnall Planet, Equivalent, if well dignified to a Fortune.

MANNERS & ACTION WHEN DIGNIFIED Very faithfull, keeping their promises with all Puncutuality, a kind of itching desire to Rule and Sway where he comes: Prudent, and of incomparable Judgment; of great Majesty and Statelinesse, Industrious to acquire Honour and a large Patrimony, yet as willingly departing therewith again; the Solar man usually speaks deliberately, but not many words, and those with great confidence and command of his own affection; full of Thought, Secret, Trusty, speaks deliberately, and nothwithstanding his great Heart, yet is he Affable, Tractable, and very humane to all people, one loving Sumptuousnesse and

Magnificence, and whatever is honourable; no sordid thoughts can enter his heart, &c.

WHEN ILL DIGNIFIED Then the Solar man is Arrogant and Proud, disdaining all men, cracking of his Pedegree, he is Pur-blind in Sight and Judgment, restlesse, troublesome, domineerning; a meer vapour, expensive, foolish, endued with no gravity in words, or sobernesse in Actions, a Spend-thrift, wasting his Patrimony, and hanging after an other mens charity, yet thinks all men are bound to him, because a Gentleman born.

CORPORATURE Usually the Sun presents a man of a good, large and strong Corporature, a yellow, saffron Complexion, a round, large Forehead: goggle eyes or large, sharp and piercing; a Body strong and well composed, not so beautiful as lovely, full of health, their hair yellowish, and there quickly bald, much Hair on their Beard, and usually an high ruddy Complexion, and their bodies fleshy, in conditions they are very bountiful honest, sincere, well-minded, of great and large Heart, High-minded, of healthful Constitution, very humane; yet sufficiently Spirited, not Loquacious.

In the Sun, we can onely say he is Orientall in the Figure, or in the Orientall quarter of the Figure, or Occidentiall, &c. all other Planets are either Orientall, when they rule, appear before him in the morning.

Occidentall, when they are seen above the Earth after he is set.

Begin Page 71

QUALITY OF MEN AND PROFESSION He signifieth Kings, Princes, Emperours, &:C. Dukes, Marquesses, Earles, Barons, Lieutenants, Deputy-Lieutenants of Countries, Magistrates, Gentlemen in generall, Courtiers, desirers of Honour and Preferment, Justices of Peace, Majors, High-Sheriffs, High-Constables, great Huntsmen, Lieutenants, Deputy-Lieutenants, Stewards of Noble-mens houses, the principall Magistrate of any City, Town, Castle or Country-Villiage, yea, though a petty Constable, where no better, or greater Officer is; Goldsmiths, Brasiers, Pewterers, Coppersmiths, Minters of Money.

SICKNESSES. Pimples in the Face, Palpitation or Trembling, or any Diseases of the Brain or Heart, Timpanies Infirmities of the Eyes, Cramps, sudden swoonings, Diseases of the Mouth, and sunking Breaths, Catars, rotten Feavers; principally in man he governeth the Heart, the Brain and right Eye, and vitall Spirit, in Women the left Eye.

COLOUR & SAVOURS. Of Colours he ruleth the Yellow, the colour of Gold, the Scarlet or the cleer Red, some say Purple: In Savours, he liketh wel a mixture of Sower and Sweet together, or Aromatical flavour, being a little Bitter and Stiptical, but withal Confortative and a little sharp.

HEARBS & PLANTS Those Plants which are subject to the Sun doe smell pleasantly, are of good flavour, their Flowers are yellow or reddish, are in growth of Majestical form, they love open and Sunshine places, their principal Vertue is to strengthen the Heart, and comfort the Vitals, to cleer the Eye-sight, resist Poyson, or to dissolve any Witchery, or Malignant Planetary Influences; and they are Saffron, the Lawrel, the Pomecitron, the Vine, Enula Campana, Saint johns-wort, Ambre, Musk, Ginger, Hearb grace, Balm, Marigold, Rosemary, Rosafolis, Cinamon, Celendine, Eye-bright, Pyony, Barley, Cinquefoile, Spikenard, Lignum Aloes, Arsnick.

TREES. Ash-tree, Palm, Lawrel-tree, the Myrrhe-tree, Frankinsence, the Cane-tree or Planet, the Cedar, Heletrepion, the Orange and Lemmon-tree.

BEASTS, &:c. The Lyon, the Horse, the Ram, the Crocodile, the Bul, Goat, Night-wormes or Glow-wormes.

FISHES The Sea-Calf or Sea-Fox, the Crabfish, the Starfish.

Begin Page 72

BIRDS. The Eagle, the Cock, the Phoenix, Nightingale, Peacock, the Swan, the Buzzard, the Slye Cantharis, the Goshawke.

PLACES. Houses, Courts of Princes, Pallaces, Theators, all magnificent Structures being clear and decent, Hals, Dining-Rooms.

MINERALS. Amongst the Elements Sun Hath domination of fire and cleer shining flames, over mettals, he ruleth Gold.

STONES. The Hyacinth, Chrisolite, Adamant, Carbuncle, the Etites stone found in Eagles nests, the Pantaure, if such a stone be the Ruby.

WEATHER. He produceth wheather according to the season; in the spring gentle moysting Showers; in the Summer heat in extremity if with Mars; in Autumn mists; in Winter small Rain.

WINDS. He loves the East part of the World; and that winde which proceeds from that quarter.

ORBE. Is 15. degrees before any aspect; and so many after separation.

YEERS. In age he ruleth youth, or when one is at the strongest; his greatest yeers are 1460, greater 120, mean 69, least 19.

COUNTRIES. Italy, Sicilia, Bohemia; and the fourth Climate, Phenicia, Chaldea.

ANGEL. Michael.

DAY OF THE WEEK & FRIENDS. He ruleth Sunday the first hour thereof, and the eight; and in numbers the first and fourth; and in conceptions the fourth moneth. His friends are all the Planets except Saturn, who is his Enemy.

Of VENUS, her generall and particular Significations.

NAME After the Sun succeedeth Venus; who is sometimes called Cytherea, Aphrodite, Phosphoros, Vesperugo, Ericina.

COLOR She is a bright shining colour, and is well known amongst the vulgar by the name of the evening Starre or Hesperus; and that is when she appears after the Sun is set: common people call he the morning Starre, and the learned Lucifer, when she is seen long before the rising of the Sun.

MOTION Her mean motion is 59 min. and 8 seconds: her diurnall motion is sometimes

Begin Page 73

62 min. a day 64, 65, 66 or 70, 74, 76 minutes; but 82 min. she never exceedeth.

LATITUDE Her greatest North or South latitude is 9 degr. and two in.in February 1643. she had eight degr. and 36 min. for her North latitude.

HOUSES She hath Taurus and Libra for her houses, she is exalted in 27 Pisces, she receiveth detriment in Aries and Scorpio, and hath her fall in 27 Virgo.

TRIPLICITY, TERMS & FACE [Note, Lilly does not use the standard Dorothean triplicity rulerships] She governeth the Earthly Triplicity by day viz. Taurus, Virgo, Capricorn; she is two dayes stationary before retrogradation, and so many before direction, and doth usually continue retrograde 42 dayes.

TERMS. She hath these degrees in every Sign for her Terms.

In ARIES, 7, 8, 9, 10, 11, 12, 13, 14.
In TAURUS, 1, 2, 3, 4, 5, 6, 7, 8.
In GEMINI, 15, 16, 17, 18, 19, 20.
In CANCER, 21, 22, 23, 24, 25, 26,27.
In LEO, 14, 15, 16, 17, 18, 19.
In VIRGO, 8, 9, 10, 11, 12, 13.
In LIBRA, 7, 8, 9, 10, 11.
In SCORPIO, 15, 16, 17, 18, 19, 20,21.
In SAGITTARIUS, 9, 10, 11, 12, 13, 14.
In CAPRICORN, 1, 2, 3, 4, 5, 6.

In AQUARIUS, 13, 14, 15, 16, 17, 18,19,20.
In PISCES, 1, 2, 3, 4, 5, 6, 7, 8.

These degrees are allowed for her Face.

In ARIES, 21, 22, 23, 24, 25, 26, 27, 28, 29, 30.
In CANCER, 1, 2, 3, 4, 5, 6, 7, 8, 9, 10.
In VIRGO, 11, 12, 13, 14, 15, 16, 17, 18, 19, 20.
In SCORPIO, 21, 22, 23, 24, 25, 26, 27, 28, 29, 30.
In PISCES, 1, 2, 3, 4, 5, 6, 7, 8, 9, 10.

Nature She is a Feminine Planet, temperately Cold and Moyst, Nocturnal, the lesser Fortune, author of Mirth and Jolity; the elements, the Ayre and Water are Venerial; in the Humours, Flegme with Blood, with Spirit, and Genital seed.

MANNERS & ACTIONS WHEN WELL DIGNIFIED She signifies a quiet man, not given to Law, Quarrel or Wrangling, not Vitious, Pleasant, Neat and Spruce, Loving

Begin Page 74

Mirth in his words and actions, cleanly in Apparel, rather Drinking much then Gluttonous, prone to Venery, oft entangles in Love-matters, Zealous in their affections, Musical, delighting in Baths, and all honest merry meetings, or Maskes and Stage-playes, easie of Belief, and not given to Labour, or take any Pains, a Company-keeper, Cheerful, nothing Mistrustful, a right vertuous man or Woman, oft had in some Jealousie, yet no cause for it.

WHEN ILL DIGNIFIED Then he is Riotous, Expensive, wholly given to Loosenesse and Lewd companies of Women, nothing regarding his Reputation, coveting unlawful Beds, Incestuous, an Adulterer; Fennatical, a meer Skip-jack, of no Faith, no Repute, no Credit; spending his Means in Ale-houses, Taverns, and amongst Scandalous, Loose people; a meen Lazy companion, nothing careful of the the things of this Life, or any thing Religious; a meer Atheist and natural man.

CORPORATURE A man of fair, but not tall Stature, his Complexion, being white, tending to a little darknesse, which makes him more Lovely; very fair Lovely Eyes, and a little black; a round Face, and not large, fair Hair, smooth, and plenty of it, and it usually of a light brown colour, a lovely Mouth and cherry Lips, the Face pretty fleshy, a rolling wandering Eye, a Body very delightful, Lovely and exceeding wel shaped, one desirous of Trimming and making himself neat and compleat both in Cloaths and Body, a love dimple in his Cheeks, a stedfast Eye, and ful amarous enticements.

ORIENTAL When Orientall the Body inclines to talnesse; or a kind of upright straightnesse in Person, not corpulent or very tal, but neatly composed. A right Venerian person, is such as we say, is a pretty, compleat, handsome Man or Woman.

OCCIDENTAL When she is Occidental, the Man is of more short stature, yet very decent and comely in Shape and Form, well liked of all.

QUALITY OF MEN & PROFESSION Musitions, Gamesters, Silk-men, Mercers, Linnen-Drapers, Painters, Jewellers, Players, Lapidaries, Embroiderers, Women-tailors, Wives, Mothers, Virgins, Choristers, Fidlers, Pipers, when joyned with Moon, Singers, Perfumers, Semilers, Picture-drawers, Gravers, Upholdsters, Limners, Glovers, all such as

Begin Page 75

sell those Commodities which adorn Women either, in Body (as Cloaths) or in Face, (as complexion-waters.)

SICKNESSES. Diseases by her signified, are principally in the Matrix and members of Generation; in the reines, belly, back, navil and those parts; the Genorrex or running of the Reines, French or Spanish Pox; any disease arising by inordinate lust. Priapisme, impotency in generation, Hernias & the Diabetes or pissing disease.

COLOUR & SAVOURS. In colours she signifieth White, or milky Skie-colour mixed with brown, or a little Green. In Savours she delightes in that which is pleasant and toothsome; usually in moyst and sweet, or what is very delectable; in smels what is unctious and Aromatical, and incites to wantonnesse.

HEARBS & PLANTS Myrtle always green; all hearbs which she governeth have a sweet flavour, a pleasant smel; a white flower; of a gentle humour, whose leaves are smooth and not jagged. She governeth the Lilly white and yellow, and the Lilly of the Valley, and of the Water. The Satyrion or Cuckoe-pintle, Maiden-hair, Violet; the white and yellow Daffadil.

TREES. Sweet Apples, the white Rose, the Fig, the white Sycamore; wilde Ash, Turpentine-tree, Olive, Sweet Oranges, Mugwort, Ladies-mantle, Sanicle-Balm, Veryin, Walnuts, Almonds, Millet, Valerian, Thyme, Ambre, Ladanum, Civet or Musk, Corriander, French Wheat, Peaches, Apricocks, Plums, Raisons.

BEASTS. The Hart, the Panther, smal cattle, Coney, the Calf, the Goat.

BIRDS Stockdove, Wagtayle, the Sparrow, Hen, the Nightingale, the Thrush, Pellican, Partridge, Ficedula, a little Bird Feeding on Grapes; the Wren, Eagles, the Swan, the Swallow, the Owse or Black Bird, the Pye.

FISHES The Dolphin.

PLACES. Gardens, Fountains, Bride-chambers, fair lodgings, Beds, Hangings, Dancing-Schooles, Wardrobes.

MINERALS, METALS & STONES Copper, especially the Corinthian and White; Brasse, all Lattenware. Cornelian, the sky-coloured Saphyre, white and red Coral, Margalite, Alabaster, Lapis Luzuli because it expels Melancholy, the Beril, Chrisolite.

Begin Page 76

WIND & WEATHER. She governeth the South-winde being hot and moyst; in the temperament of the Ayre, she ruleth the Etesia; she foretelleth in Summer, Serenity or cleer weather; in Winter, rain or snow.

ORBE. Her Orbe is 7. before and after any aspect of hers.

YEERS. Her greatest yeers are 151. her greater 82. her mean 45. her least 8. In man she governeth Youth from 14 to 28.

COUNTRIES. Arabia, Austria, Campania, Vienna, Polonia the greater, Turing, Parthia, Media, Cypress, and the six climate.

ANGEL. Her Angel is Anael.

DAY OF THE WEEK & FRIENDS. Her day of the week Friday, of which she rules the first and eighth houre; and in conception the first Month. Her Friends are all the Planets except Saturn.

Of MERCURY, his generall and particular Significations.

NAME He is called Hermes, Stilbon, Cyllenius, Archas. Mercury is the least of all the Planets, never distant from the Sun above 27.degrees; by which reason he is seldom visible to our sight:

COLOR He is of a dusky silver colour; his mean motion is 59 min. and 8 seconds; but he is sometimes so swift that he moveth one degree and 40.min. in a day, never more; so that you are not to marvaile if you finde him sometimes goe 66. 68. 70. 80. 86. or 100. in a day: he is Stationary one day, and retrograde 24.dayes.

LATITUDE His greatest South Latitude is 3.degr. 35.min. His greatest North Latit. is 3.deg. 33.min.

HOUSES He hath Gemini and Virgo for his Houses, and is exalted in the 15. of Virgo: he receives detriment in Sagittarius and Pisces, his fall is in Pisces.

TRIPLICITY, TERMS & FACE [Note, Lilly does not use the standard Dorothean triplicity rulerships] He ruleth the aery triplicity by night, viz. Gemini, Libra, Aquarius.

TERMS. He hath these degrees in every Sign for his Terms.

In ARIES, 15, 16, 17, 18, 19, 20, 21.
In TAURUS, 9, 10, 11, 12, 13, 14, 15.
In GEMINI, 1, 2, 3, 4, 5, 6, 7.
In CANCER, 14, 15, 16, 17, 18, 19, 20.
In LEO, 7, 8, 9, 10, 11, 12, 13.
In VIRGO, 1, 2, 3, 4, 5, 6, 7.

Begin Page 77

In LIBRA, 20, 21, 22, 23, 24.
In SCORPIO, 22, 23, 24, 25, 26, 27.
In SAGITTARIUS, 15, 16, 17, 18, 19, 20.
In CAPRICORN, 7, 8, 9, 10, 11, 12.
In AQUARIUS, 7, 8, 9, 10, 11, 12.
In PISCES, 15, 16, 17, 18, 19, 20.

FACE. These subsequent degrees are his Faces or Decanate:

In TAURUS, 1, 2, 3, 4, 5, 6, 7, 8, 9, 10.
In CANCER, 11, 12, 13, 14, 15, 16, 17, 18, 19, 20.
In VIRGO, 21, 22, 23, 24, 25, 26, 27, 28, 29, 30.
In SAGITTARIUS, 1, 2, 3, 4, 5, 6, 7, 8, 9, 10.
In AQUARIUS, 11, 12, 13, 14, 15, 16, 17, 18, 19, 20.

Nature We may not call him either Masculine or Feminine, for he is either the one or other as joyned to any Planet; for if in Conjunction with a Masculine Planet, he becomes Masculine; if with a Feminine, then Feminine, but of his own nature he is cold and dry, and therefore Melancholly; with the good he is good, with the evil Planets ill:

ELEMENTS. In the Elements the Water; amongst the humours, the mixt, he rules the animal spirit: he is author of subtilty, tricks, devices, perjury, &c.

MANNERS & ACTIONS WHEN WELL DIGNIFIED Being wel dignified, he represents a man of a subtil and politick brain, intellect, and cogitation; an excellent disputant or Logician, arguing with learning and discretion, and using much eloquence in his speech, a searcher into all kinds of Mysteries and Learning, sharp and witty, learning almost any thing without a Teacher; ambitious of being exquisite in every Science, desirious naturally of travel and seeing foraign parts: a man of an unwearied fancy, curious in the search of any occult knowledge; able by his own Genius to produce wonders; given to Divination and the more secret knowledge; if he turn Merchant, no man exceeds him in a way of Trade or invention of new wayes whereby to obtain wealth.

WHEN ILL DIGNIFIED A troublesome wit, a kinds of Phrenetick man, his tongue and Pen against every man, wholly bent to spoil his estate and time in prating and trying nice conclusions to no purpose; a great lyar, boaster, pratler, busibody, false, a tale-carrier, given to wicked ARTS, as Necromancy, and such like ungodly

Begin Page 78

knowledges; easie of beleef, an asse or very ideot, constant in no place or opinion, cheating and theeving every where; a news-monger, pretending all manner of knowledge, but guilty of no true or solid learning; a trifler; a meer frantick fellow; if he prove a Divine, then a meer verball fellow, frothy of no judgment, easily perverted, constant in nothing but idle words and bragging.

CORPORATURE Vulgarly he denotes one of an high stature and straight thin spare body, an high forehead and somewhat narrow long face, long nose; fair eyes, neither perfectly black or gray, thin lips and nose, little hair on the chin, but much on his head, and it a sad brown inclining to blacknesse; long arms, fingers and hands; his complexion like an olive or Chestnut colour. You must more observe Mercury then all the Planets; for having any aspect to a Planet, he doth more usually partake of the influence of that Planet then nay other doth: if with Saturn then heavy, with Jupiter more temperate, with Mars more rash, with Sun more genteele, with Venus more jesting, with Moon more shifter.

ORIENTAL When he is oriental, his complexion is honey colour, or like one wel Sun-burnt; in the stature of his body not very high, but wel joynted, smal eyes, not much hair; in very truth, according to the the height of body, very wel composed, but stil a defect in the complexion, viz. swarty brown, and in the tongue, viz. all for his own ends.

OCCIDENTAL When Occidental, a tawny visage, lank body, small slender limbs, hollow eyes, and sparkling and red or fiery; the whole frame of body inclining to drinesse.

QUALITY OF MEN & PROFESSION He generally signifies all literated men, Philosophers, Mathematicians, Astrologians, Merchants, Secretaries, Scriveners, Diviners, Sculptors, Poets, Orators, Advocates, School-masters, Stationers, Printers, Exchangers of Money, Atturneys, Emperours, Embassadours, Commissioners, Clerks, Artificers, generally Accomptants, Solicitors, sometimes Theeves, pratling muddy Ministers, busie Sectaries, and they unlearned; Gramarians, Taylors, Carriers, Messengers, Foot-men, Userers.

SICKNESSES. All Vertigols, Lethargies or giddinesse in the Head, Madnesse, either Lightnesse, or any Disease of the Brain; Ptisick, all

Begin Page 79

stammering and imperfection in the Tongue, vein and fond Imaginations, all defects in the Memory, Hoarcenesse, dry Coughs, too much abundance of Spettle, all snaffling and snuffling in the Head or Nose; the Hand and Feet Gout, Dumnesse, Toungue-evil, all evils in the Fancy and intellectual parts.

COLOUR & SAVOURS. Mixed and new colours, the Gray mixed with Sky-colour, such as is on the Neck of the Stock-dove, Linsie-woolsie colours, or consisting of many colours mixed in one. Of Saviours an hodgepodge of all things together, so that no one can give it any true name; yet usually such as doe quicken the Spirits, are subtil and penetrate, and in a manner insensible.

HEARBS & PLANTS Herbs attributed to Mercury, are known by the various colour of the flower, and love sandy barren places, they bear their seed in husks or cobs, they smel rarely or subtilly, and have principal relation to the tongue, brain, lungs or memory; they dispel winde, and comfort the Annimal spirits, and open obstructions.

Beanes, three leaved-grasse, the Walnut and Walnut-tree; the Filbert-tree and Nut; the Elder-tree, Adders-tongue, Dragon-wort, Twopenny-grasse, Lungwort, Anniseeds, Cubebs, Marjoran. What hearbs are used for the Muses and Divination, as Vervine, the Reed; of Drugs, Treacle, Hiera, Diambra.

BEASTS. The Hyaena, Ape, Fox, Squirrel, Weasel, the Spider, the Grayhound, the Hermophradite, being partaker of both sexes; all cunning creatures.

BIRDS. The Lynnet, the Parrot, the Popinian, the Swallow, the Pye,the Beetle, Pifinires, Locusts, Bees, Serpent, the Crane.

FISHES The Forke-fish, Mullet.

PLACES. Tradesmens-shops, Markets, Fayres, Schooles, Common Hals, Bowling-Allyes, Ordinaries, Tennis-Courts:

METALS Quicksilver.

STONES. The Milestone, Marchasite or fire-stone, the Achates, Topaz, Vitroil, all stones of divers colours.

WIND & WEATHER. He delights in Windy, Stormy and Violent, Boistrous Weather, and stirs up that Wind which the Planet signifies to which he applyes; sometimes Rain, at other times Haile, Lightning, Thunder and Tempests- in hot Countries Earthquakes, but this

Begin Page 80

must be observed really from the Sign and Season of the year.

ORBE. His Orbe is seven degrees before and after any aspect.

YEERS. His greatest yeers are 450; his greatest 76; his mean 48; his little or least 20: in Conceptions he governeth the sixth moneth.

COUNTRIES. He hath Grecia, Flanders, Egypt, Paris.

ANGEL. His Angel is named Raphael.

DAY OF THE WEEK & FRIENDS. He governeth Wednesday, the first hour thereof, and the eight. His Friends are Jupiter, Venus, Saturn and his Enemies all the other Planets.

Of the MOON, her generall and particular Significations.

NAME The Moon we find called by the Ancients, Lucina, Cynthia, Diana, Phoebe, Latona, Noctiluca, Prosperpina; she is neerest to the Earth of all the Planets; her colour in the Element is vulgarly known:

MOTION. She finisheth her courte through the whole twelve Signs in 27 days, 7 hours and 43 min. or thereabouts: her mean motion is 13 degr. 10 min. and 36 seconds, but she moveth sometimes lesse and sometimes more, never exceeding 15 degr. and two min. in 24 hours space.

LATITUDE Her greatest North Latitude is 5 degr. and 17 min.(or thereabouts) Her greatest South Latitude is 5 degr. and 12 min. (or thereabouts) She is never Retrograde, but always direct; when she is slow in motion, and goeth lesse in 24 hours then 13 degr. and 10 min. she is then equivalent to a Retrograde Planet.

HOUSE She hath the Sign Cancer for her house, and Capricorn for her detriment; she is exalted in 3. Taurus, and hath her fal in 3 grad. Scorpio; she governeth the Earthly Triplicity by night, viz. Taurus, Virgo, Capricorn.

TRIPLICITY, TERMS & FACE [Note Lilly does not use the standard Dorothean triplicity rulerships] The Sun and she have no Terms assigned them.

In the twelve Signs she hath these degrees for her Decanate or Face.

In TAURUS, 11, 12, 13, 14, 15, 16, 17, 18, 19, 20.
In CANCER, 21, 22, 23, 24, 25, 26, 27, 28, 29, 30.

Begin Page 81

In LIBRA, 1, 2, 3, 4, 5, 6, 7, 8, 9, 10.
In SAGITTARIUS, 11, 12, 13, 14, 15, 16, 17, 18, 19, 20.
In AQUARIUS, 21, 22, 23, 24, 25, 26, 27, 28, 29, 30.

NATURE She is Feminine, Nocturnal Planet, Cold, Moyst and
Flegmatique.

MANNERS & ACTIONS WHEN WELL DIGNIFIED She
signifieth one of composed Manners, a soft, tender creature, a Lover
of all honest and ingenuous Sciences, a Searcher of, and Delighter in
Novelties, naturally propense to frit and shift his Habitation,
unstedfast, wholly caring for the present Times, Timorous, Prodigal,
and easily Frighted, however loving Peace, and to live free from the
cares of this Life, if a Mechannick, the man learnes many
Occupations, and frequently will be tampering with many wayes to
trade in.

WHEN ILL DIGNIFIED A meer Vagabond, idleperson, hating
Labour, a Drunkard, a Sot, one of no Spirit or Forecast, delighting to
live beggarly and carefly, one content in no condition of Life, either
good or il.

CORPORATURE She generally presenteth a man of fair stature,
whitely coloured, the Face round, gray Eyes, and a little Touring;
much Hair both on the Head, Face, and other parts; usually one Eye
a little larger then the other; short Hands and fleshy, the whole Body
inclining to be fleshy, plump, corpulent and flegmatique: if she be
impedited of the Sun in a Nativity or Question, she usually signifies
some blemish in, or neer the Eye: a blemish neer the Eye, if she be
impedited in Succedant Houses; in the Sight, if she be unfortunate in
Angles and with fixed Starres, called Nebulose.

QUALITY OF MEN & PROFESSION She signifieth Queens,
Countesses, Ladies, all manner of Women; as also the common
People, Travellers, Pilgrims, Sailors, Fishermen, Fish-mongers,
Brewers, Tapsters, Vintners, Letter-carriers, Coach-men, Hunts-men,
Messengers, (some say the Popes Legates) Marriners, Millers, Ale-
wives, Malstors, Drunkards, Oister-wives, Fisher-women, Chare-
women, Tripe-women, and generally such Women as carry

Commodities in the Streets; as also, Midwives, Nurses, &c, Hackney-men, Water-men, Water-bearers.

SICKNESSES. Apoplexies, Palsie, the Chollick, the Belly-ache, Disease

Begin Page 82

in the Left Side, Stones, the Bladder and members of Generation, the Men-stries and Liver; in Women Dropsies, Fluxes of Belly, all cold Rheumatick Diseases, cold Stomack, the Gout in the Rists and Feet, Sciatica, Chollick, Worms in Children and men, Rheumes or Hutts in the Eyes, viz. in the Left of Men, and Right of Women: Sursets, rotten Coughs, Convultion fits, the Falling sicknesse, Kings-evil, Apostems, smal Pox and Measels.

COLOUR & SAVOURS. Of Colours the White, or pale Yellowish White, pale Green, or a little of the Silver-colour. Of Saviours, the Fresh, or without any flavour, such as is in Hearbs before they be ripe, or such as doe moysten the Brain, &C.

HEARBS & PLANTS Those Hearbs which are subject to the Moon have soft and thick juicy leaves, of a waterish or a little sweetish taste, they love to grow in watry places, and grow quickly into a juicy magnitude; and are. The Colwort, Cabbage, , Melon, Gourd, Pompion, Onion, Mandrake, Poppy, Lettice, Rape, the Linden-tree, Mushroomes, Endine, all Trees or Hearbs who have round, shady, great spreading Leaves, and are little Fruitful.

BEASTS & BIRDS All such Beasts, or the like, as live in the water; as Frogs, the Otter, Snailes, &c. the Weasel, the Cunny, all Sea Fowls, Coockoe, Geese and Duck, the Night-Owle.

FISHES The Oyster and Cockle, all She-fish, the Crab and Lobster, Tortoise, Eeles.

PLACES. Fields, Fountains, Baths, Havens of the Sea, Highwayes and Desertplaces, Port Towns, Rivers, Fish-ponds, standing Pools, Boggy places, Common-shoars, little Brooks, Springs.

METALS Silver.

STONES. The Selenite, all soft Stons, Cristals.

WEATHER. With Saturn cold Ayre; with Jupiter Serene; with Mars Winds red Clouds; with the Sun according to the Season; with Venus and Mercury Showres and Winds.

WIND In Hermetical operation, she delighteth towards the North, and usually when she is the strongest Planet in the Scheam, viz. in any Lunation, she stirs up Wind, according to the nature of the Planet she next applies unto.

Begin Page 83

ORBE. Is 12. degrees before and after any Aspect.

YEERS. Her greatest yeers are 321. greater 108. mean 66, least 25. in conceptions she ruleth the seventh moneth.

COUNTRIES. Holland, Zealand, Denmarke, Norimberge, Flanders.

ANGEL. Gabriel.

DAY OF THE WEEK Her day is Monday the first hour and the eight, after the rise of the Sun.

The Nodes of the Moon [Note: the North Node of the Moon is known as the Cauda Draconis, the Head of the Dragon and the South Node as the Cauda Draconis, the Tail of the Dragon. The Nodes are the points where the orbit of the Moon intersects the Ecliptic, the orbit of the Sun.]

The Head of the Dragon is Masculine, of the nature of Jupiter and Venus, and of himself a Fortune; yet the Ancients doe say, that being in Conjunction with the good he is good, and in conjunction with the evil Planets they account him evil.

The Tayle of the Dragon is Feminine by Nature, and clean contrary to the Head; for he is evil when joyned with good Planets, and good when in conjunction with the malignant Planets. This is the constant opinion of all the Ancients, but upon what reason grounded I know not; I ever found the North Node equivalent to either of the Fortunes, and when joyned with the evil Planets to lessen their malevolent signification; when joyned with the good to increase the good promised by them:

For the Tayle of the Dragon, I always in my practise found when he was joyned with the evil Planets; their malice or the evil intended thereby was doubled and trebled, or extreamly augmented, &c. and when he chanced to be conjunction with any of the Fortunes who were significators in the question, though the matter by the principal significator was fairely promised, and likely to be perfected in a smal time; yet did there ever fal out many rubs and disturbances, much wrangling and great controversie, that the businesse was many times given over for desperate ere a perfect conclusion could be had; and unlesse the principal significators were Angular and wel fortified with essential dignities, many times unexpectedly the whole matter came to nothing.

APPENDIX C

PLANETARY HOUR ELECTIONS FROM THE KEY OF SOLOMON

the Greater Key of Solomon, translated by S. Liddell Macgregor Mathers

BOOK I CHAPTER II

OF THE DAYS, AND HOURS,
AND OF THE VIRTUES OF THE PLANETS

When thou wishest to make any experiment or operation, thou must first prepare, beforehand, all the requisites which thou wilt find described in the following Chapters : observing the days, the hours, and the other effects of the Constellations which may be found in this Chapter. It is, therefore, advisable to know that the hours of the day and of the night together, are twenty-four in number, and that each hour is governed by one of the Seven Planets in regular order, commencing at the highest and descending to the lowest.

...It must, therefore, be understood that the Planets have their dominion over the day which approacheth nearest unto the name which is given and attributed unto them-viz., over Saturday, Saturn; Thursday, Jupiter; Tuesday, Mars ; Sunday, the Sun; Friday, Venus ; Wednesday, Mercury; and Monday, the Moon. It must, therefore, be understood that the Planets have their dominion over the day which approacheth nearest unto the name which is given and attributed unto them-viz., over Saturday, Saturn; Thursday, Jupiter; Tuesday, Mars ; Sunday, the Sun; Friday, Venus ; Wednesday, Mercury; and Monday, the Moon.

The rule of the Planets over each hour begins from the dawn at the rising of the Sun on the day which takes its name from such Planet, and the Planet which follows it in order, succeeds to the rule over the next hour. Thus (on Saturday) Saturn rules the first hour, Jupiter the second, Mars the third, the Sun the fourth, Venus the fifth, Mercury the sixth, the Moon the seventh, and Saturn returns in the rule over the eighth, and the others in their turn, the Planets always keeping the same relative order. Note that each experiment or magical operation should be performed under the Planet, and -usually in the hour, which refers to the same. For example :-

TIMING OF MAGIC BY
THE PLANETARY DAYS & HOURS

In the Days and Hours of Saturn thou canst perform experiments to summon the Souls from Hades, but only of those who have died a natural death. Similarly on these days and hours thou canst operate to bring either good or bad fortune to buildings ; to have familiar Spirits attend thee in sleep ; to cause good or ill success to business, possessions, goods, seeds, fruits, and similar things, in order to acquire learning ; to bring destruction and to give death, and to sow hatred and discord.

The Days and Hours of Jupiter are proper for obtaining honours, acquiring riches ; contracting friendships, preserving health ; and arriving at all that thou canst desire.

In the Days and Hours of Mars thou canst make experiments regarding War ; to arrive at military honour ; to acquire courage ; to overthrow enemies ; and further to cause ruin, slaughter, cruelty, discord ; to wound and to give death.

The Days and Hours of the Sun are very good for perfecting experiments regarding temporal wealth, hope, gain, fortune, divination, the favour of princes, to dissolve hostile feeling, and to make friends.

The Days and Hours of Venus are good for forming friendships; for kindness and love ; for joyous and pleasant undertakings, and for travelling.

The Days and Hours of Mercury are good to operate for eloquence and intelligence ; promptitude in business ; science and divination ; wonders ; apparitions ; and answers regarding the future. Thou canst also operate under this Planet for thefts; writings; deceit; and merchandise.

The Days and Hours of the Moon are good for embassies; voyages envoys; messages; navigation; reconciliation; love; and the acquisition of merchandise by water. Thou shouldest take care punctually to observe all the instructions contained in this chapter, if thou desirest to succeed, seeing that the truth of Magical Science dependeth thereon.

The Hours of Saturn, of Mars, and of the Moon are alike good for communicating and speaking with Spirits; as those of Mercury are for recovering thefts by the means of Spirits.

The Hours of Mars serve for summoning Souls from Hades, especially of those slain in battle.

The Hours of the Sun, of Jupiter, and of Venus, are adapted for preparing any operations whatsoever of love, of kindness, and of invisibility, as is hereafter more fully shown, to which must be added other things of a similar nature which are contained in our work.

The Hours of Saturn and Mars and also the days on which the Moon is conjunct with them, or when she receives their opposition or quartile aspect, are excellent for making experiments of hatred, enmity, quarrel, and discord; and other operations of the same kind which are given later on in this work.

The Hours of Mercury are good for undertaking experiments relating to games, raillery jests, sports, and the like.

The Hours of the Sun, of Jupiter, and of Venus, particularly on the days which they rule, are good for all extraordinary, uncommon, and unknown operations.

The Hours of the Moon are proper for making trial of experiments relating to recovery of stolen property, for obtaining nocturnal visions, for summoning Spirits in sleep, and for preparing anything relating to Water.

The Hours of Venus are furthermore useful for lots, poisons, all things of the nature of Venus, for preparing powders provocative of madness and the like things. But in order to thoroughly effect the operations of this Art, thou shouldest perform them not only on the Hours but on the Days of the Planets as well, because then the experiment will always succeed better, provided thou observest the rules laia down later on, for if thou omittest one single condition thou wilt never arrive at the accomplishment of the Art.

MAGICAL TIMING BY THE MOON

For those matters then which appertain unto the Moon, such as the Invocation of Spirits, the Works of Necromancy, and the recovery of stolen property, it is necessary that the Moon should be in a Terrestrial Sign, viz. :-Taurus, Virgo, or Capricorn.

For love, grace, and invisibility, the Moon should be in a Fiery Sign, viz. :-Aries, Leo, or Sagittarius.

For hatred, discord, and destruction, the Moon should be in a Watery Sign, viz. :-Cancer, Scorpio, or Pisces.

For experiments of a peculiar nature, which cannot be classed under any certain head, the Moon should be in an Airy Sign, viz. :-Gemini, Libra, or Aquarius.

But if these things seem unto thee difficult to accomplish, it will suffice thee merely to notice the Moon after her combustion, or conjunction with the Sun, especially just when she quits his beams and appeareth visible. For then it is good to make all experiments for the construction and operation of any matter. That is why the time from the New unto the Full Moon is proper for performing any of the experiments of which we have spoken above. But in her decrease or wane it is good for War, Disturbance, and Discord. Likewise the period when she is almost deprived of light, is proper for experiments of invisibility, and of Death. But observe inviolably that thou commence nothing while the Moon is in conjunction with the Sun, seeing that this is extremely unfortunate, and that thou wilt then be able to effect nothing; but the Moon quitting his beams and increasing in Light, thou canst perform all that thou desirest, observing nevertheless the directions in this Chapter.

TIMING FOR INVOCATION

Furthermore, if thou wishest to converse with Spirits it should be especially on the day of Mercury and in his hour, and let the Moon be in an Airy Sign, as well as the Sun. Retire thou then unto a secret place, where no one may be able to see thee or to hinder thee, before the completion of the experiment, whether thou shouldest wish to work by day or by night. But if thou shouldest wish to work by night, perfect thy work on the succeeding night ; if by day, seeing that the day beginneth with the rising of the Sun (perfect thy work on) the succeeding day. But the Hour of Inception is the Hour of Mercury.

APPENDIX D

PLANETARY RITUAL PREPARATIONS FROM PICATRIX

from *Picatrix*, Book III, chapter 7

SATURN

And when Saturn is dignified and in a good place, and you wish to speak and pray to him, wrap yourself in black clothing, namely the clothing which is used for a corpse, and also a black cloak of a doctor, and wear black shoes.

Then go to a place that is appropriate for the work, like a place that is remote and humble, if you wish you can go to a place of the Jews, because Saturn rules them (literally is the lord of their conjunction).

On your hand have an iron ring, and carry an iron censer [incense burner] with you, with burning charcoal placed in it, throw into it the mixture for suffumigation, the form of whose composition is this: Take opium, saffron, actarag (this is an herb) the seed of laurel, carui, wormwood, dry wool, coloquintide, and the head of a black cat in equal parts. Combine everything completely and mix in the urine of black she-goat; and make it into portions (literally threads).

And when you wish to do the work put some on the burning charcoal in the censer and save some, and turn towards Saturn, and while the smoke rises from the censer say your invocation.

JUPITER

When you wish to speak to Jupiter. When you wish to speak to Jupiter, place him in a good state as we have said with Saturn. Then wear yellow and white clothing, then go to a place for the work that is remote and safe that resembles the place of a hermit or is a place of Christians, [be] girded with a belt with a ring of crystal in the [shape of a] cross on your finger and wearing a white cloak.

And take a censer made of a Jovial metal and place burning fire in it. And in this way you make the suffumigation: namely take classe, storax, the feet of a dove, peony, aromatic calamus, resin, pine and the seeds of hellebore in equal parts. Mix thoroughly and add pure old wine (namely of many years) and make out of it pills.

And when you wish to work as we have said throw the pills into the fire in the censer. And turn around in the direction of the heavens where Jupiter is and say [the invocation of Jupiter].

MARS

When you wish to pray to Mars. When you wish to make a request of Mars and to speak and honor him, place him in a good state as we have said before about Saturn.

And wear red clothing, and on your head [wear] red linen or silk or place a red hat on your head. And strengthen yourself with all kinds of weapons, and equip yourself as a fighter or soldier, and place a bronze ring on your finger.

And take a bronze censer and burn charcoal and place your suffumigation in it. Take absinthe, aloe, [lemon grass?] euphorbium, allspice, lesser cress, in equal parts. Mix everything with the blood of a man. Make pills from this and put it aside to use.

And when you wish to begin working, place the [pills of incense] in the censer, and carry it to a remote place that it is appropriate [to Mars]. And when you have reached [the place of the working] stand on your feet and secretly audacious and without fear turn to the south toward Mars who should be fortunate and in a good state as we have said before, always looking upon him. And as the smoke rises say [the invocation].

THE SUN

When you wish to pray to the Sun. When you wish to pray to the Sun and to ask for thing like the grace of a king or the love of lords, and to acquire power, make the Sun fortunate an place him in the Ascendant in his day and hour.

And wear royal clothing, silk with yellow and gold mixed, and place a gold crown on your head, and wear a gold ring on your finger, in the form of a great man of the Chaldeans, because the Sun is ruler of the Chaldeans (literally, the lord of their Ascendant). And go to a house that is separate and set aside for your work, and place your right hand over your left and look modestly at the Sun, and your appearance should be modest and bashful.

Then take your gold censer and have a beautiful rooster by the neck, above the neck place a small wax candle, and on the head place the branch of a large palm tree, and in the fire of the censer place the suffumigation. And raise the rooster towards the Sun and as the fumes from the censer rise say [the invocation]:

Note, Picatrix goes on to say that the suffumigation of the Sun is policarie, bdellium, myrrh, laudanum, enule, old siseleos, Celtice, Indian poli, old clean pine, cardomelle, cardamon, aromatic calamus, incense, husk of muscate nut, dried roses, saffron, the spice nard, caper root, pentafilon, aromatic hoof (?) balsam seeds, epithimi, squinati, gourd seeds, eastern spice plant, terebinth, pulverised dates, raisin wine, and honey mixed with wine.

VENUS

When you wish to pray to Venus. When you wish to pray to Venus and ask for the things that pertain to her, look to see that she is far from the malefics, direct and not retrograde and fortunate.

Put on the first or second styles and the best one is the robe and trappings of a noble Arab man. Wear white clothes and white cotton on your head because this is his [signature or seal]. Another style is that of woman. Wear long clothes of silk and gold mixed, precious and beautiful and on your head place a crown richly adorned with precious stones and pearls and on your hand a gold ring with pearls and on your arms wear bracelets of gold; in your right hand hold a mirror and in your left hand a comb. Put before you a jug of wine and in your clothing place crushed aromatics and odoriferous [incense or scent] in the way that women do.

Then take a censer made of gold and silver mixed and place burning charcoal in it, throw the suffumigation into it. And as the fumes rise say the invocation.

Picatrix goes on to say that the suffumigation of Venus is lignum aloes, a rooster, costi, saffron, laudanum, mastic, poppy seed husks, willow leaves and lily root in equal parts. Mix thoroughly with rose water and make pills of incense.

MERCURY

When you wish to pray to Mercury. When you wish to pray to Mercury and you wish to ask for things appropriate to him which are petitions to scribes and kings and regarding rulership.

Dress as if you were a notary or scribe, the Moon conjoining Mercury, and in every way act as if you were a scribe and wear a ring of Mercury mortified [?] that is a ring with an [image] of Hermes [Trismegistus] for the work. And sit on a throne similar to the throne of a judge, and turn your face towards it [?], with a [book or paper] in your hand looking like you wish to write.

And have incense appropriate to Mercury and place the suffumigation in the fire. And as the fumes rise, say the invocation.

Picatrix goes on to say that the incense of Mercury is composed of oak, cumin, dried gariofilate, myrtle branches, bitter almond husks, gum arabic, tamarind seed, grape vine, squinanti, in equal parts. Mix with pure and delicate wine and make into pills.

THE MOON

When you wish to pray to the Moon. When you wish to pray to the Moon and ask for that which pertains to her, dress yourself in the fashion of a young man and wear something that smells good and in your hand have a ring of silver and your movement and work should be smooth and elegant and your speech distinguished, in a good style and to the point.

And have in front of you a censer of silver. And on the 14 day of the lunar month, so long as the Moon is above the earth and making a good aspect with the Benefics, wash your face and turn towards [the Moon] and say the invocation.

Picatrix goes on to say that the suffumigation of the Moon is mastic, cardamon, savin, storax, cardelli pepper, enule, myrrh, dar sessahal, lily root, Celtice, Indian poli, pine cones, laudanum, dried roses, ayrob, raisin wine, grape mixed with very subtle wine, make pills about the size of a chickpea.